COSTUMES AND ORNAMENTS OF CHAMBA

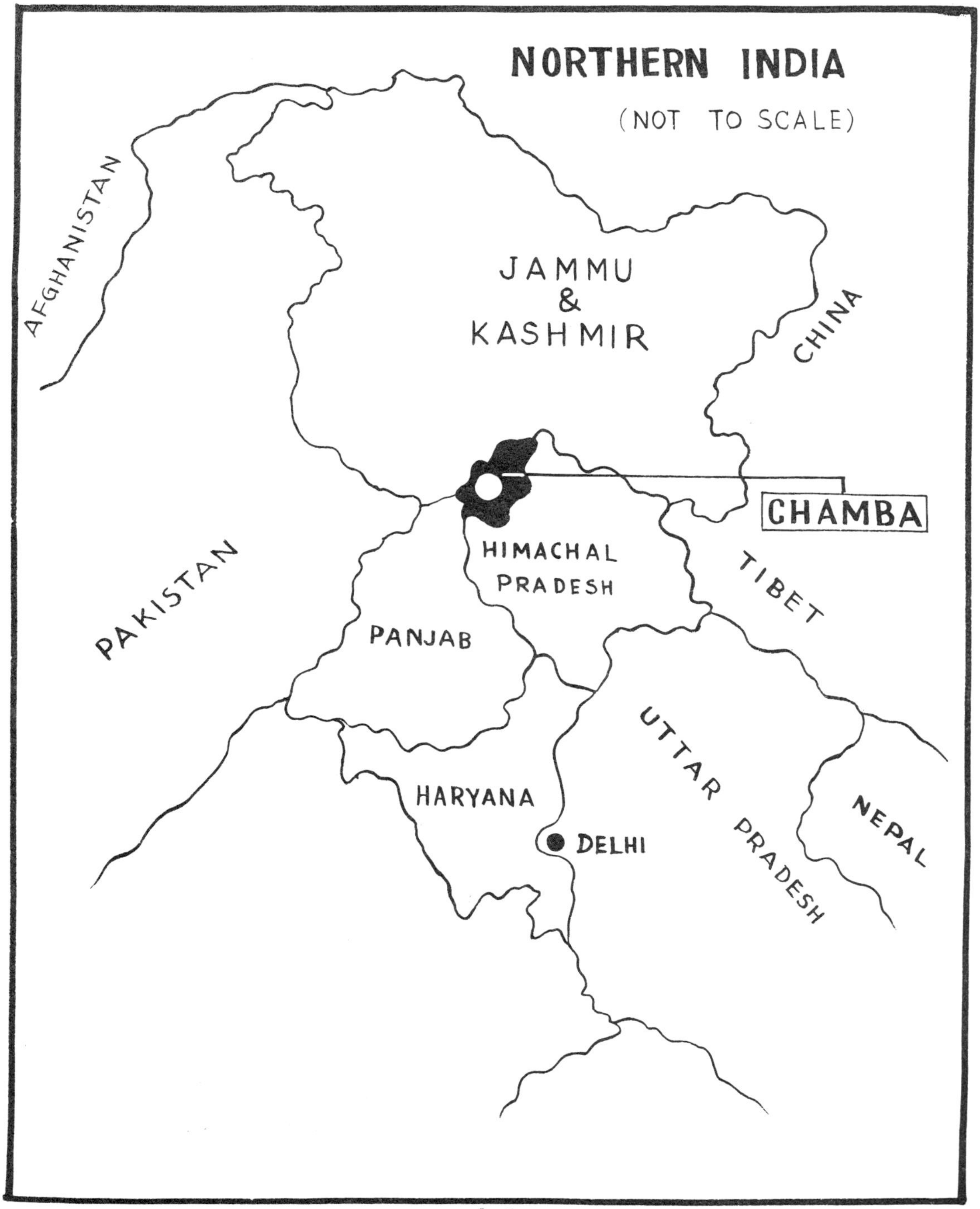

Map showing the location of Chamba district.

COSTUMES AND ORNAMENTS OF CHAMBA

KAMAL PRASHAD SHARMA
SURINDER MOHAN SETHI

INDUS
INDUS PUBLISHING COMPANY
NEW DELHI

ISBN 81-7387-067-5

Published by M.L. Gidwani, Indus Publishing Company
FS-5, Tagore Garden, New Delhi 110 027, and printed at
Elegant Printers, Mayapuri Indl. Area, New Delhi

Dedicated to the people of
Chamba

Contents

Foreword 15

Preface 21

Part I—Costumes

Chapter 1. INTRODUCTION 27

1. Chamba: Location and physical features
2. Chamba: A brief history
3. Costumes
4. Costumes of Chamba: Earliest references
5. Process of cloth-making
6. Chamba costumes: Historical perspective

Chapter 2. COSTUMES OF GADDIS 44

1. Gaddis
2. The land of Gaddis
3. Gaddi way of life
4. Costumes of Gaddis (men)
5. Costumes of Gaddans (women)

Chapter 3. COSTUMES OF GUJJARS 56

1. Gujjars
2. Chamba Gujjars
3. Costumes of Gujjars (men)
4. Costumes of Gujjaris (women)

Chapter 4. COSTUMES OF PANGWĀLĀS 63

1. Pangwālās
2. Costumes of Pangwālās (men)
3. Costumes of Pangwālans (women)

Chapter 5. COSTUMES OF CHURĀHĪS 69

1. Churāhīs
2. Costumes of Churāhīs (men)
3. Costumes of Churāhans (women)

Chapter 6. COSTUMES OF CHAMBYĀLS 75

1. Chambyāls
2. Costumes of Chambyāls (men)
3. Costumes of Chambyālans (women)

Chapter 7. COSTUMES OF BHAṬṬIYĀLS 83

1. Bhaṭṭiyāls
2. Costumes of Bhaṭṭiyāls (men)
3. Costumes of Bhaṭṭiyālans (women)
4. Costumes of Gurkhas (Nepalis)

Part II—Ornaments

Chapter 8. ORNAMENTS 91

Chapter 9. ORNAMENTS FOR HEAD, EARS, NOSE AND NECK 95

1. Ornaments for head
2. Ornaments for ears
3. Ornaments for nose
4. Ornaments for neck

Chapter 10. ORNAMENTS FOR UPPER ARMS, WRISTS AND FINGERS 110

1. Ornaments for upper arms
2. Ornaments for wrists
3. Ornaments for fingers

Chapter 11. ORNAMENTS FOR ANKELS, TOES, FOR MALES AND OTHER DECORATIVE PIECES 115

1. Ornaments for ankels
2. Ornaments for toes
3. Ornaments for males
4. Other decorative pieces

Chapter 12. CONCLUSION (Both Parts) 120

Appendices

1. Tribes and people of Chamba 124
2. Costumes worn by inhabitants of different tehsils of Chamba 126
3. Ornaments worn by different people and tribes of Chamba 129
4. Costumes in Pahāḍi paintings 133

References 135

Index 136

PRONUNCIATION

The authors have followed an adaptation of the International Phonetic Script for transcription of Vernacular sounds. The adaptation followed is indicated below:

Vowels (= स्वर)

a (= अ)	ā (= आ)	i (= इ)	ī (= ई)
u (= उ)	ū (= ऊ)	ṛ (= ऋ)	ḷ, lr (= लृ)
e (= ए)	ai (= ऐ)	o (= ओ)	au (= औ)
aṇ (= अं)	ah (= अः)		

Consonants (= व्यंजन)

k (= क)	kh (= ख)	g (= ग)	gh (= घ)	ṅ (= ङ)
ch (= च)	chh (= छ)	j (= ज)	jh (= झ)	ñ (= ञ)
ṭ (= ट)	ṭh (= ठ)	ḍ (= ड)	ḍh (= ढ)	ṇ (= ण)
t (= त)	th (= थ)	d (= द)	dh (= ध)	n (= न)
p (= प)	ph (= फ)	b (= ब)	bh (= भ)	m (= म)
y (= य)	r (= र)	l (= ल)	v (= व)	
sh, ś (= श)	ṣh, ṣ (= ष)	s (= स)	h (= ह)	

List of Plates

A1. Female figures from fountain stone slab of Churāh, 11th cent. A.D. revealing stitched garments resembling *choli* and *ghāgrā* (Courtesy Bhuri Singh Museum, Chamba).

A2. Needles of sheep or goat-bones and musk-deer fangs.

A3. Lady spinning wool on *charkhā*.

A4. Weaving *paṭṭu* (woollen cloth) on family handloom known as *rachh*.

A5. Bronze image of master sculptor Guggā (7th century A.D.) (Courtesy Bhuri Singh Museum, Chamba).

A6. Figure of a donor in Indo-Scythian dress, resembling with Gaddi *cholā* (over-coat), *ṭop* (peaked cap), *suthan* (trousers) (Kushān sculpture, Mathura Museum).

A7. Figures from fountain stone slab, 11th century A.D., donning dress faintly resembling Scythian garments (Courtesy Bhuri Singh Museum, Chamba).

A8. Carved figure of Raja Prithvi Singh of Chamba (1641-1664 A.D.) on wooden door showing him in Mughal costume and holding royal insignia of fish known as a māhī-o-marātib (Courtesy Bhuri Singh Museum, Chamba).

A9. Painting of Wazir Bagha in Sikh costume shown with Gaddi petitioner (mid-19th century A.D.) (Courtesy Bhuri Singh Museum, Chamba).

A10. A Gaddi functionary of the State.

A11. A Gaddi wearing a *ṭop* (peaked cap).

A12. A Gaddi couple in their traditional dress.

A13. *Baglu* (leather bag) with *ruṇkā* (flint-lock).

A14. *Jaḍulā* (goat-hair boots).

A15. Gaddi women husking paddy with wooden clubs known as *mohal*.

A16. A Gaddi belle in her traditional finery.

A17. Decorative mirror to be fastened on the *ḍora*.

A18. A Gujjar kid wearing a peculiar cap having a peaked top, called Gujjari *ṭopi*.

A19. A Gujjar in his traditional dress.

A20. A Gujjar woman in her traditional dress.

A21. A Gujjar lady wearing a head-dress called *joji*.

A22. A Pangwālā in his traditional dress.

A23. Traditional dress of a Pāngi woman.

A24. Cap worn by Pāngi women known as *joji*.

A25. Straw shoes called *pulān*.

A26. Embroidered laced leather foot-wear and leather socks known as *mozā* and *chappal* (Courtesy Bhuri Singh Museum, Chamba).

A27. Group photograph of Churāhī women in their tribal costumes.

A28. Ceremonial dress worn in Chamba proper (*sāfā, chogā, pyjāmā*).

A29. Embroidered leather foot-wear known as *paṇi* (Courtesy Bhuri Singh Museum, Chamba).

A30. Two ladies, one wearing printed skirt known as *ghāgrā* and other wearing long over-coat known as *peshwāj*.

A31. Chamba costume *peshwāj* and *dupaṭṭā*.

A32. Embroidered bodice known as *choli*.

A33. Group photograph showing the residents of Bhaṭṭiyāt with musical instruments.

A34. A woman in black *ghāgrā*.

A35. A woman of Bhaṭṭiyāt with her children.

A36. A Gaddi lady donning silver and gold ornaments.

B1. Feathers made as decorative curls, *kunḍals*, for fastening to the hair.

B2. Nitika wearing ornaments of dry fruits for Lohri festival.

B3. String having beads which ward off evil eye called *nazar-baṭṭu* or *kunḍhu*.

B4. Head ornament which is braided in hair known as *chaunk* and *phull*.

B5. Plait to be worn over combed hair above the forehead called *singārpaṭṭi*.

B6. Round forehead ornament known as *chiḍi*.

B7. Forehead ornament *chiḍi* fastend to hair plait, *singārpaṭṭi*.

B8. Round forehead ornament known as *chilkainwala manṭikā*.

B9. Crescent-shaped forehead ornament called *argh-chandru*.

B10. Chain called *janjeer* or *shangli*.

B11. Ear ring known as *bāle*.

B12. Ear rings which are put arround the ear called *kālu* or *kāḍu*.

B13. Flower-shaped ear stud fastened to hair with chain called *karaṇ-phul*, suspended lobe attached to the *karaṇ-phul* makes it a pair of *lurku*.

B14. Big round ear stud called *pharālu*.

B15. Cap-shaped ear ornament called *jhumkā*.

B16. Prominent nose ring called *bālu*.

B17. Nose ring, central piece is made by joining five pipal leaves known as *chutkiwālā bālu*.

B18. Ornament which is suspended from the septum of the nose called *balākḍu* or *ḍoḍā-balāk*.

B19. Nose pin with prominent face called *long*.

B20. Ring which is suspended from the septum of nose called *nathli*.

B21. Necklace which has bud-like pieces strung in the thread called *chamkali* or *jaumālā* (Courtesy Bhuri Singh Museum, Chamba).

B22. Necklace which has round piece like soapnut called *ḍoḍmālā*.

B23. Ornament having three rows of small beads worn tightly on the neck called *kanṭhṇu*.

B24. Broad strip meant for decorating the neck, made up by joining enamelled pieces with hooks to parallel threads known as *gulband* or *guluband* (Courtesy Bhuri Singh Museum, Chamba).

B25. Heart or leaf-shaped or a round pendant which is fitted with coloured stones called *nām*.

B26. Necklace with square pendant containing a painting of Śiva *parivār* called *sabihi* (Courtesy Bhuri Singh Museum, Chamba).

B27. Squar pendant known as *tabeet*.

B28. The *chanderhār* to be worn in neck.

B29. Sickle-shaped neck ornament called *hansli* or *sahiri*.

B30. Necklace in which old coins are strung to the thread called *mhail* or *hamail*.

B31. Small pendant having figures of deceased person called *auttar*.

B32. A cylindrical hallow capsule made into a pendant by means of hooks called *ḍhol* or *ḍhaḍi*.

B33. Bangle for the upper arm called *nant*.

B34. Broad wrist ornament called *bajuband*.

B35. Heavy bracelets having lion head-ends called *kangṇū*.

B36. A variation of *kangṇū* known as *gokhru*.

B37. Hollowed bangles known as *maredaḍi* or *gōjru*.

B38. Wrist bangles, gold bar is interlaced and ends have lion-mouth called *kangṇū* (*kangaṇ*).

B39. A type of designed bangles called *ṭoke*.

B40. Wrist bangles provided with jingling *bores* called *chhaṇ-kangaṇ*.

B41. Wrist strap called *ponchhi* (Courtesy Bhuri Singh Museum, Chamba).

B42. Finger rings in different designs.

B43. Ring for the thumb with a mirror called *arsi*.

B44. Ornament for fore-finger called *nahastrā* (Courtesy Bhuri Singh Museum, Chamba).

B45. A popular ankle ornament with cluster of jingling balls called *panjeb*.

B46. Delicately designed ankle ornament called *toḍā*.

B47. Hollowed and designed ankle ornament called *jhānjhar*.

B48. Toe ring called *porḍi*.

B49. Silver buttons and chain.

B50. Three-stringed *mālā* of silver beads.

B51. Coiled bar for the ears called *dur*.

B52. Scent box called *attar-dāni*.

B53. Horse hair bangles and finger rings (Courtesy Bhuri Singh Museum, Chamba).

B54. An elderly Gujjar woman wearing a traditional jewellery.

FOREWORD

Clothing is considered as one of the three basic necessities of mankind alongwith food and shelter. But even while thinking about the primitive man, food perhaps is the only basic requirement to sustain life. Researchers and anthropologists have confirmed that the evolving man did not require any covering or clothing like his nearer cousins and neighbours, i.e. monkeys and apes. It cannot, however, be denied that the evolving man governed by the instincts of self-preservation also learnt, later on, the use of caves, boughs, tree-hollows, as well as barks, skins and clothes. Yet no student of cultural anthropology believes that an important tradition like clothing evolved purely on utilitarian grounds. Darwin established even in the 19th century that our warm and cosy garments could not be a basic requirement for human beings. He had seen snow melting over the bodies of the primitives of 'Tera Del-Fugo' with hardly any concern by them.

Similarly, modesty leading to the covering of primary and secondary sex characteristics has also been rejected as the other basic motivating factor for the evolution of clothing. Researches have established that auto-exhibitionism is the quality of human mind which acts as a catalytic agent for the evolution of all kinds of costumes and ornaments. A child of an year or two loves and insists to exhibit his nudity in the first place. Without any concern for nudity he may, however, decorate his body with leaves, flowers, earth-colours, papers and pieces of cloth motivated by his instinctive urge and sense of exhibitionism. It is only under the social and parental insistence that he accepts at a much later stage, clothes as a social habit and a necessity.

With the sexual attraction rising to somewhat emotional and psychological levels in developing mankind, the significance of primary and secondary sex characters started being recognised. Public exhibition of these characters was considered more important than other parts of the body. It was exhibition of these characters which has primarily been responsible for the wearing of fig-leaves and tattooing in the first instance, and to the wearing of skirts, bodices, and all other modern elongative and projectile coverings later on. Auto-exhibitionism of physical power also led the hunter to wear teeth, nails, plumes, skins and firs of his prize as trophies of the prowess. The same exhibitionism led to the wearing of head-gear of enemy skulls, strings of enemy fingers and heads, and looted arms of the fallen foe. Use of these heroic trophies or their symbolic replicas as protective talismans 'and decorative agents was just the simple next step in human evolution.

Exhibition of primary and secondary sex characters has already been cited. Similarly, wearing of trophies as mark of one's prowess has also been indicated. These trophies in the course of time became decorative motifs within one's own community, whereas they served as awe-inspiring objects for evil spirits and enemies. Then different modes of clothings evolved in different tribes in accordance with their physical environment.

They also came to be identified as marks of one's profession, occupation and social standing. Different cuts and modes of costumes and varieties of ornamentation also served the purpose of showing one's material prosperity. Expansion of wearer's personality also got unconsciously associated with the wearing of clothes, ornaments and such other embellishments. Clothes with padded shoulders, padded hips and padded breasts, as also big caps, hats, turbans and such other broad-rimmed, horned, coned, plumed or elongated head-gear that enhanced the height and stature of the wearer served the psychological feeling of one's biological being to be extended upto the ends of these coverings. Similarly, long gowns of kings and queens, etc. subconsciously served as means of psychological expansion of one's being in the early stages of evolution of mankind.

In modern times, protection, modesty, and the most important aspect of exhibitionism, as manifest through decoration and social distinction, as also the aesthetic consideration have all synthesised in the wearing of clothes and ornaments. Quick changes in the fashions of costumes and ornamentation these days also clearly indicate that protection probably is the more unimportant of the factors for their use as compared to the urge of exhibitionism. Progressive prevalence of nudism, semi-nudism, topless and bottomless wearings, use of tight-fitting garments, use of mostly uncomfortable and painful ornaments in fashions also subscribe to the opinion of modesty also being secondary to the urge of decoration and auto-exhibitionism.

In undertaking the study of costumes and ornaments of any people it is in fact an endeavour of unfolding the total cultural evolution of that area and its inhabitants, which the learned scholars of this volume have ventured in.

The study of costumes and ornaments of Chamba is all the more a challenging as well as a rewarding effort. Chamba as a political and cultural entity has had the distinction of remaining more exclusive than most areas in India mostly due to its geographical location. This exclusiveness has mainly been responsible for the preservation in their original or near original form all manifestations of human endeavour including all cultural, literary and artistic expressions. This feature of the region was further reinforced by the continued rule of a single dynasty over the state for as long as 12 centuries with almost undisturbed political boundaries. This uninterruption causes the accumulation of human experience in an unbroken chain and in a steady tradition. All this makes study of any aspect of the life of Chamba and its people a very rich and rewarding experience. But this exclusiveness also serves as a big disadvantage and bottleneck because generally no source material or cross-references about the old times are available. Scholars, historians or chronologers from outside were perhaps hardly able to have any access to such exclusive areas and experiences. As such, one has mostly to depend on the extant material on the one hand, and the local traditions and beliefs on the other. Though the local traditions and beliefs in any exclusive society are reasonably authentic, yet in the evolutionary process many simple facts get converted into cultural and social symbols, motifs, and metaphors, the deciphering of which into authentic meaning poses another serious problem.

Mr. Kamal Prashad Sharma and Mr. Surinder Mohan Sethi have accepted this challenge boldly and tried to provide answers to a number of problems related to Chamba and its people by trying to unfold their uninterrupted tradition of costumes and ornaments over the centuries. The learned scholars have made no claim to deeper anthropological, historical or art-historical research through this volume. But they have really undertaken a more important and basic scholarly work, i.e. collection and preservation of the basic source material, leading to and helpful in multi-dimensional research at a later stage. In the fast changing world of today even the most exclusive areas like Pāngi are fast opening up to external influences. The fast process of mobilisation, i.e. increasing migration and cross-migration of people for administrative, political, commercial, educational and professional purpose have opened up and changed almost any and every society howsoever remote or exclusive it may have been. Easy availability of alternatives is also an important factor for change in human habits. The influx of readymade materials have almost totally disrupted the use of traditional indigenous materials and manufacturing processes of the local costumes and ornaments. Within decades it has been observed that certain objects which were in use for centuries in a specific form just vanished or got unrecognisably transformed. It is quite likely that within another few decades the old and the traditional forms of these objects may totally vanish or may get fully transformed. It is the duty of the society and its designated institutions, such as the museums, to preserve the authentic samples of these important social-historical source materials. The authors of this volume have really done a great service to the cause of human knowledge by trying to catalogue, classify and analyse the costumes and ornaments of Chamba in the context of its different geographical regions, various castes, diverse classes and varied professional groups. They have also tried to hint at the direct or indirect external influences, such as access of or proximity to the Mughal court or Sikh court of a certain Chamba prince, or the spread of Vaiśnava influence in the valley etc. for the use of certain kind or kinds of dresses in Chamba. Scanty as these hints and references may be, I believe, they are sure to go a long way in helping the future and prospective researchers in the fields of cultural and social history of the region who undertake to unfold the past of this land and its people. I wish to personally express my deep appreciation and gratitude to the twin scholars. I also undertake to congratulate and thank the duo on behalf of the people of Chamba in general and all those researchers, present and prospective, engaged in the study of cultural history of India, for their significant work.

MAITHILI PRASAD BHARADWAJ
Sr. Professor
Dept. of Hindi
Punjab University,
Chandigarh

PREFACE

Nowhere else in India the Costumes and Ornaments of the tribals are so exotic, colourful and divergent as happens to be the case in Chamba, because Chamba has remained secluded and remote for centuries, and it was able to preserve its rich art and cultural heritage.

Many art historians like Hermann Goetz were induced to remark that the costumes of Gaddis were strikingly similar to the Indo-Scythian donor figures found in Kushāna art of 2nd century B.C. The Gujjars of today are the remnants of the lost Gurjara-Pratihara empire of 7th-8th century A.D., and their criss-cross embroidery techniques can be traced to the tribal folks of Baltis, Hunzas of Hindukush and Kafiristan regions, from where once the Gurjara-Barbarian hordes had descended on the crumbled Gupta empire.

The fountain-stone-slabs of Chamba are replete with scores of quaint donor figures and the fallen warriors wearing dresses and costumes long discarded by the civilized world. But it used to be the dress once worn by the men and women of the Gurjara folk.

The ornaments of Chamba are so varied and different in variety that it has been a difficult task for us to bring all of them into a single book. The work of documentation of different designs and types of ornaments posed still more problems. The goldsmiths of Chamba, who since many generations have been casting traditional ornaments, have all been very well-known to us, yet they have been either too much immersed in their work, or have been reluctant to reveal secrets of their family traits. It required a lot of coaxing and cajoling on our part to have some useful information out of them.

We did not come across any reference book on the costumes and ornaments of Chamba to bank upon. We were often left on our own to go to and rely on primary sources and objects. We, however, got on with field investigations and surveys, the subject went on opening itself and the sailing became quite smooth.

This book has been divided into two parts. The first part relates to Costumes of Chamba and the second part to the Ornaments of Chamba.

Though the volume is slim yet it has been our endeavour to pack it with as much information as possible, and we are hopeful that even a casual reader will find in it some or the other thing of interest to him. We have been working on the subject for the last over ten years. For some time the incomplete manuscript was tossed in a corner of the shelf, due to one problem or the other. But the subject lay steady in our minds in whatever state the mind was and in whatever conditions we were.

Now the work is before the enlightened readers. We have no claim to be complete and perfect. Even if a handful of readers and scholars of the subject find some thing of interest in it, we will feel amply rewarded for this—our life-time's labour

Acknowledgements

The profound love for Chamba and its people induced Dr. M.P. Bharadwaj, Sr. Professor, Department of Hindi, Punjab University, Chandigarh, to write Foreword of this book. We are indebted to him.

To Professor Vijay Mohan Sethi, Post-graduate College, Dharamsala (H.P.), we reserve our special thanks. He has been very kind to edit our manuscript, which presented many problems regarding maintaining uniformity of language and an easy readable style. Our thanks are also due to Mr. Nandesh Kumar, Curator, Bhuri Singh Museum, Chamba for reading the text and providing some rare photographs of ornaments.

To our friend Mr. Lakshmi Prashad Sharma, District Librarian, Chamba, we express our deepest gratitude for all the encouragement and guidance provided by him.

To late Mr. Amar Chand Soni and Mr. Achharo Ram Soni, two of the most prominent goldsmiths of Chamba, we offer our heartfelt thanks. They very generously spent hours together with us sharing their knowledge of the subject of ornaments.

We are grateful to Mr. Om Prakash of Photo Studio, Chamba and Mr. Rajneesh (Raju) a college student for the pictorial section. Our thanks are due to Mr. Suresh Mahajan for all his encouragement and help due to which we have been able to produce this book.

We are thankful to Mr. Nanak Chand Dharmani for sharing his knowledge about Pāngi, the remotest area of Chamba, which is included in this book. We are also thankful to Mr. Devender Baglwan for typing the manuscript with deep love and care.

Quite a few of the ladies and gentlemen of Chamba willingly came forward to share information and offer invaluable hints which immensely helped in giving this book its present form. We hardly find suitable words to adequately express our appreciation and gratitude for all of them. We sincerely say that we feel greatly indebted to them.

We are thankful to Indus Publishing Co. who have taken great care to bring out this book.

K.P. Sharma
S.M. Sethi

Part I
Costumes

1

Introduction

1. Chamba: Location and Physical Features

Situated in the extreme north-west of the State of Himachal Pradesh, Chamba district is stretched between the upper Ravi (Vedic name—Purūṣṇi) valley and Chandra-Bhaga (Vedic name—Asikni) valley between north latitude 32° 10′ and 33° 13′ and east longitude 75° 45′ and 77° 33′ with an estimated area of 6,92,419 hectare. The district is surrounded on all sides by lofty hill ranges and the altitude in this entire mountainous territory ranges between 2,000 and 21,000 feet above sea level. Mountain systems and ranges in association with river basins determine the natural division of the district, which happens to be the most important factor in the evolution of cultural diversity and the resultant great variety in the sartorial habits and traits of its inhabitants. The main and the central region of Chamba lies between the watershed of Dhaula-Dhār and that of Pir Panjāl and constitutes the drainage area of the Ravi river and its tributaries and three important sub-divisions of Brahmour, Chamba and Churāh. The basin of Chandra-Bhaga (Chenab) and its tributaries, ensconced between the mountain ranges of Pir Panjāl and Zaskar, forms the second important region of the district known as Pāngi valley and constitutes the northern-most Pāngi sub-division of the district. The southernmost territory of Chamba relates to the basin of river Beas, which river in fact does not flow through Chamba district. But three tributaries of Beas namely Chakki, Dairh and Brāhl form the catchment area over that part of the district known as Bhaṭṭiyāt sub-division, which lies between the Dhaula-Dhār range of mountains and the Hathi-Dhār range of lower hills.

Chamba is bounded on the north-west and west by Jammu and Kashmir; on the north-east and east by Ladakh area of Jammu and Kashmir State and Lahul and Bara Banghal areas of Himachal Pradesh; on the south-east and south by the district of Kangra of Himachal Pradesh, and Gurdaspur district of Punjab. Chamba is surrounded by huge snow-peaked mountains of the intermediary zone of the western Himalaya. These mountains have always stood as watchdog not only against the attacks of the foreigners from the plains, but also from the invaders of high mountain lands like Tibet, etc. This perhaps is the most important reason for the propagation and preservation of a distinct life-style and a rich art and cultural heritage, almost intact in its undiluted and unadulterated form even upto the present times.

2. Chamba: A Brief History

An effort to briefly delineate the history of Chamba may be highly relevant to this work. Evolution of the use of costumes and ornaments is part of the process of human culturisation. It is through history alone that the growth and development of a people interacting in their geographical locale with the internal and external forces can be underlined. History of Chamba may help in throwing light on the historical forces, the external settlers, the foreign invaders, the natural cultural fusion and synthesis with the neighbouring groups of people, and all the more the changing life and cultural styles of the ruling classes that caused the evolution and wider use of varied costumes and ornaments of this area.

The origin of Chamba is not known definitely but it came into existence around 6th century A.D. out of the turmoils caused by the invasions of Huns and other tribes from north-west of India and consequent disintegration of the Gupta empire. Nucleus of the State was the present Brahmour—Brahmapura of the ancient times as mentioned by Vrahmihira in *Bṛhatsaṁhita*. The territory at the time was divided into diminutive states known as Raṇhu or Thakurie in possession of Ranas, Rajanakas, Thakurs and Samantkas. Expansion of the Brahmour kingdom occurred after Raja Sahila Verman subjugated these petty chieftains in 10th century A.D. and shifted his new capital from Brahmour to Chamba. Even prior to the reign of Raja Sahila Verman, Chamba (Champak-pur, Champa) was in existence in some form or the other as revealed by archaeological evidence in the form of the foundation of a 6th century A.D. brick temple of the late Gupta period.[1] Also the idol of Hari Rai (Vaikunṭh-murti) in Hari Rai temple of Chamba town, which is still under worship, belongs to 8th century A.D. A Surya image recovered between Chamba valley and Brahmour, wearing Indo-Scythian costume and squatting in Kushāna fashion belongs to 6th century A.D., and bears some Gupta influence.[2]

Great grammarian Panini also mentions the name of Champa, Chamba (ca. 5th century B.C.) on the northern side of Kulut (Kulu) on the valley of Chandra-Bhaga (Chenab).

Regarding the early history of this region it is believed that this area was at one time inhabited by a certain Kolian tribe,[3] which was subjugated later by the Khāśas. The Khāśas too after a time (around 2nd cent. B.C.) came under the sway of Audumbaras. The Audumbaras had republican form of government and worshipped Śiva as their principal deity. According to Hermann Goetz:

> "The Audumbaras were Mongoloid Khāśas who had subjected the older primitive Koli tribes. Orthodox Hindus regarded them as degraded Kshatriyas. They venerated

1. Now in the collection of Bhuri Singh Museum, Chamba.
2. Now in the collection of Bhuri Singh Museum, Chamba.
3. General Cunningham believed that the western Himalaya was at one time occupied by a true Kolian group from the same race as the Kolis of Central India. There was also probably a large Dravidian element in the aboriginal population of hills. T.S. Negi, Gazetteer of Chamba (1963), p. 87.

> snake deities (Nagas) and demons (Yakshas and Rakshasas) and a cruel mother goddess demanding human sacrifices; today the Nagas are often identified with Rishis, and the female demon or the cruel goddess with Hidimba (Hirma) of the Mahabharata or Chamunda."[1]

From the Gupta period (4th century A.D.) the Chamba region was under the control of Thakurs and Ranas who considered themselves superior to the low tribes of Kolis[2] and Khāśas. According to Hermann Goetz:

> "By the middle of the 6th century, the Śūlikas, a people from Central Asia associated with the Gurjaras, overran northwestern India, but were defeated by the Maukharis and founded the vassal Kingdom of Brahmapura which extended from Kumaon to the Chenab. Its first capital was at Talesvar in Kumaon which after the death of Harashavardhana was destroyed by the Tibetans under Sron-btsaṇsgam-po. Thereafter Meruvarman, the scion of another Śūlika dynasty, founded Brahmapura Brahmor in Chamba which early in the 8th century became a vassal of Kashmir, lost its Śūlika-Gurjara character because of considerable transfer of population by Lalitāditya-Muktāpīḍa of Kashmir and was destroyed by a second Tibetan invasion under Khari-Sron-Ide-btsan in the later 8th century."[3]

German scholar Hermann Goetz further writes:

> "Advised by the Kāṇphata saint Charpata, probably a successor of the Siddhacharya Charpaṭi Nātha, guru of Meruvarman (?), and his eighty four Yogis, he introduced Pratihara civilization and art."[4]

---

1. Hermann Goetz, *Studies in the History and Art of Kashmir and the Indian Himalaya*, Wiesbaden (1969), p. 129.
2. Even now 30% of population of Himachal Pradesh is constituted by the Kolis.
3. Hermann Goetz, *Studies in the History and Art of Kashmir and the Indian Himalaya*, Wiesbaden (1969), p. 130.
4. Ibid., p. 135.

The German art-critic further elaborates:

> "In the 10th century A.D. the fortunes of the fallen Brahmor dynasty were restored by Sahilavarman (ca. A.D. 920-940), the founder of Chamba State. He seems to have risen as a general of the Pratiharas, who became military governor of the mountain frontier against the encroachments of Kashmir under Śaṁkaravarman (A.D. 883-902) and, thereafter, of the Hindu Sahis of Kabul who, first vassals of Kashmir, soon became independent rulers of the Punjab."[1]

According to Dr. B.N. Puri:

> "The evidence available from a few inscriptions and the artistic influence on temples and sculptures reveal Pratihara or Gurjara-Pratihara impact, both political and cultural, on Chamba and its rulers."[2]

With the rise of Gurjara-Pratiharas, the Rajput dynasties came to power in Chamba which had great impact on the life-style of this area.

According to genealogy or Vaṁśāvalī (*bansauli*) of Chamba rulers, in c. 550 A.D. a legendary hero called Maru migrated to the north-west from Kalāpa-grāma[3] and founded Brahmpura (Brahmour) in the valley of the Budhal river, about 75 kilometres upstream to

---

1. Hermann Goetz, *Studies in the History and Art of Kashmir and the Indian Himalaya*, Wiesbaden (1969), p. 135.
2. 'Chamba under Gurjara-Pratiharas', A research paper read by Dr. B.N. Puri, Emeritus Professor, Lucknow in an international seminar at Chamba.
3. Kalāpa-grāma: A village where Maru and Devapi, the last kings of the Solar and Lunar races respectively performed asceticism to re-appear again as kings of Ayodhya and Hastinapura by Kalki, the tenth incarnation of Vishnu (Kalki Purana, Pt. III, Ch. 4).

   Kalāpa-grāma appears to have been situated on the Himalaya near Badrikāshrama. In the Vayu Purana (Ch. 91) Kalāpa is placed among the Himalayan countries where Urvashi passed some time with Pururava. According to Capt. Raper, Kalāpa-grāma is near the source of the Sarasvati, a tributary of the Alaknanda in Badrinath in Garhwal. Nandu Lal Dey, *The Geographical Dictionary of Ancient and Medieval India*, New Delhi (1971), p. 84.

the east of Chamba. His successors continued to rule over the country from the capital city for over 300 years until Sahila Varman shifted his capital from Brahmapura to the more centrally located plateau in the lower Ravi valley. It is said that he named the town after his beloved daughter Champa. He planned the town on the right back of the river as prescribed by the ancient archaeological or *Vastu-Shilpa* codes of the Aryans. His queen Naina Devi voluntarily offered herself as a sacrifice to get the water to the town-folk through a running channel which takes origin at a place called Bhalotha. The layout of the plan of Chamba seems to be in conformity with the ancient Hindu texts. From then on, the rajas of Chamba continued to rule from here in an uninterrupted and direct line of descent till India's independence in 1947 and the creation of the State of Himachal Pradesh.

Chamba is the only state in northern India to preserve a well documented history from circa 550 A.D. onwards. Its high mountain ranges gave it a sheltered position and helped in preserving its centuries-old relics and numerous inscriptions. The temples erected by rajas of Chamba more than a thousand years ago continue to be under worship and the land-grant deeds (*Paṭṭas*) executed by them on copper plates continue to be valid under the law.

The state was never invaded by Muslims. Its cultural heritage and folk tradition have thus remained undamaged, uninterrupted and unbroken. It has, however, its occasional fights with the neighbouring states in the hills with similar cultural background. As such, the damage to Chamba from these invasions was seldom serious and never beyond the possibility of repair. During the Mughal rule north India experienced comparatively peaceful conditions. These were the times when the popularity of Vaiśnavism was spreading. It spread over these remote hills also. Akbar tried to extend a loose control over the hill states including Chamba, and attached fertile tracts of these states to the Imperial territory. Aurangzeb once issued orders to the Raja of Chamba, Chattar Singh (1664-1694 A.D.) to pull down the beautiful temples of

Chamba. But, instead the Raja in clear defiance to the Mughal ruler placed gilded pinnacles or *Kalashas* on these temples. He was thereupon ordered to come down to Delhi to face the imperial wrath. But Aurangzeb himself had to leave for the Deccan war from where he could not disengage himself till the end of his life. On the whole, the northern India experienced comparatively peaceful conditions during the Mughal regime. Raja Prithvi Singh (1641-1664 A.D.), a handsome and a gallant knight was favourite of Shahjahan, and visited the Imperial court many times. He introduced the Mughal style of court life including Mughal-Rajput art and architecture in Chamba.

The years between 1752 and 1758 A.D. of the reign of Raja Umed Singh were the happiest period in the context of Chamba. Umed Singh had been educated at the Mughal court and thus he grew up into a refined and accomplished young prince. Consequent upon the collapse of the Mughal empire a large number of administrators, artists, artisans and scholars from the Imperial court and the courts of provincial rulers became refugees and therefore were easily available. This providence introduced the renaissance of Mughal tradition of art, culture, administration and general life-style during the early 18th century in the existing principalities of the region including Chamba. In Chamba, Raja Prithvi Singh had introduced far-reaching administrative reforms which were further consolidated and completed by Umed Singh. In other social and cultural activities also Chamba State saw a period of great reforms and innovation during the period.

By the last quarter of 18th century the Sikhs in Punjab forced the hill states to pay tribute to them. Maharaja Ranjit Singh systematically deposed the hill princes including the more powerful Kangra ruler Sansar Chand Katoch. Chamba, however, was spared on account of the services rendered by Wazir Nathu of Chamba to the Maharaja on two occasions. In 1809 A.D. the Wazir had made himself useful to the Maharaja by negotiating an agreement with the aforementioned Raja Sansar Chand Katoch of Kangra. Again in

1817 A.D. he had saved Ranjit Singh's life by offering his own horse to the Maharaja at a critical moment during former's winter campaign in Kashmir. After Ranjit Singh's death, however, Chamba also became unprotected and was drawn into the vortex of disintegration of the Sikh kingdom. The Sikh army invaded the British territory in 1845 A.D. and the troops of Sikh army which were stationed at Chamba were withdrawn. When Sikhs were defeated it was decided to merge Chamba in Jammu and Kashmir but on account of the timely intervention of another ingenious Wazir Bagha of Chamba it was taken directly under the British control and subjected to an annual tribute of Rs. 12,000. The rajas who saw, lived and worked under the British hegemony were Sri Singh, Gopal Singh, Sham Singh, Bhuri Singh, Ram Singh and Lakshman Singh till the independence of India. Their relations with the British political officers remained all through very cordial, and, Chamba witnessed great many reforms and made significant progress during this period. On 15th April 1948, the new State of Himachal Pradesh was formed within Indian Union by merging four principal States of Chamba, Mandi, Suket and Sirmur and all the other two dozen odd states of Shimla Hills.

In all, there have been about 67 rajas who ruled over Chamba starting from Raja Maru who is believed to have founded the Brahmour principality in 6th century A.D. It seems to be a unique case in India where one dynasty continued to rule the state from 6th century onward till its merger into the Republic of India in 1947. Prior to Raja Sahila Varman, Chamba State, which is now called the Chamba district, was not a unified much less a single administrative unit initially, there being several petty rulers called Ranas. The Ranas occupied under their rule bits and parts of the present territory as more or less independent political and administrative entities. These almost autonomous fiefdoms were called Raṇhu. The next phase in the administrative history commenced with the advent of Raja Sahila Varman who subjugated the numerous petty Ranas, and founded an integrated territorial entity which came to function more or less as a unit under the supreme control of one ruler. His successors further consolidated their domain and established the well-demarcated state as it more or less existed for over 1200 years.

The Chamba rajas divided the whole of the state into five *Manḍalas*, later on known as *Wazarats*. These *wazarats* or administrative provinces have been—Chamba, Brahmour, Bhaṭṭi (or Bhaṭṭiyat), Churāh and Pāngi. This division was based on the location of each region exclusive from the other regions due to high mountains, deep rivers and thick forested tracts. This topographical exclusiveness caused the evolution of highly varied dialects, life-styles, costumes, ornaments, fairs, festivals, dietary habits and other social and cultural manifestation in all the five regions of the state. From the point of view of this study this natural division of a single administrative district in five distinct regions is quite significant because the costumes and ornaments of Chamba have been conventionally and strictly available in their regional characteristics and can be distinctly classified in five broad categories.

3. Costumes

It is presumed that the use of dress began when the pre-historic man joined leaves together with the flowers for decorating his body. The study of dresses reveals that it was decoration of the human body, which was the chief motivation for clothing among the primitive people rather than the instinct of modesty. The material available about costumes in Vedic literature is so scanty that it is difficult to come to any conclusion. It is mentioned in the Vedas that the regions through which Indus and Purūṣṇi (Ravi) flowed, produced dyed or bleached woollen stuff—*sundhyavah*. *Pusān* is said to be raiment from the wool of sheep. From the wool, obtained from these countries were manufactured blankets—*kambalā*. Panini in Ashṭādhyāyī refers to the art of preparing of blankets and needle work in the country of Audumbaras. According to Hermann Goetz:

"Also the Panjab Himalaya had since olden times been famous for its textile industry. The Jatakas, the Milinda Pañha and the Vinaya of the Mūlasarvāstivādins mention the beautifully embroidered Kotumbara clothes of the Audumbara country ('Pathankot and Chamba'), and the fine textiles captured in the lot of Kangra Fort A.D. 1009 aroused the astonishment of the soldiers of Mahmud of Ghazni. A heavier, though not less luxurious type of embroidered dresses can be traced on the fountain stones which had been erected by the local aristocracy of Churāh (western Chamba) in the 11th and 12th centuries."[1]

4. Costumes of Chamba: Earliest References

Pesas in Vedic literature was worn by dancing girls and was perhaps the earliest form or forerunners of modern *peshwāj*. Charles Fabri suggests that the *peshwāj* was the first stitched garment introduced in the hills (16th century A.D.).[2] The study of numerous fountain stone slabs erected and found in Churāh and Pāngi areas of Chamba district (11th to 13th century A.D.) reveal the stitched garments faintly resembling the *choli* (bodice) and *ghāgrā* (skirt) worn by the figurines engraved on these slabs. The *Nāṭya Śāstra* of Bharat Muni[3] underlines the wearing of different kinds of dresses for different occasions. The famous Chinese travellers, Yuan-Chwang and I-tsing also mention in their travelogues (4th to 6th century A.D.) the stitched garments in use by the people of Kashmir and other colder regions.[4]

It is striking to note that the Gaddis of Brahmour, Pangwālās of Pāngi, and even Churāhīs of upper Churāh, still use the bone-needles excavated in Mohenjo-daro and Harappa sites (1500 to

---

1. Hermann Goetz, *Rajput Art and Architecture*, edited by Jyotindra Jain Jutta Jain, Neubauer, Wiesbaden (1978), p. 190.
2. Charles Louis Fabri, *Indian Dress: A Brief History*, New Delhi (1960), p. 23.
3. The period of Nāṭya Śāstra mentioned by various scholars ranges between the Vedic age to 7th century A.D.
4. *Marg*, Vol. XXXIII, No. 1, p. 34.

2000 B.C.). The Gaddis of Brahmour still use a particular type of needle called *saṇān* or *bak-suā* made from bones of sheep or goat. In the later Vedic period, cloth made from hemp is mentioned as *saṇ*, probably the *saṇān* is derived from the word *saṇ*. The *bak-suā* or *saṇān* is used in sewing *thālch* (broad or tape-shaped rope) and *jaḍulā* (long boots) made from goat's hair. In the remote Pāngi valley of Chamba, the long and sharp fangs of musk deer are also used for preparing needles called *saṇān*. These needles are coarse and thick, and are used for sewing the articles prepared from goat's hair like *thobi* (mat) and *rajuḍ*[1] (flat tape-rope). It is quite possible that in early times this type of needle was used in preparing the dresses of this area. Elders of the region also confirm the fact that in medieval times the Gaddis and Pangwālās stitched their garments with bone needles. The *bak-suā* of iron made by local blacksmiths, known as Rehāḍās, which is long coarse needle is still used for sewing their garments. Bhupendra Nath Dutta writes:

> "The Rig-Veda speaks of needles (Suchi). Hence, tailor-made or sewn garments for the upper part of the body or for the covering of the whole body must have existed from the Vedic days. Ghurge admits that it is not denied that tailored garments for the upper part of the male body were known before the Gupta period and even from the Vedic time."[2]

5. Process of Cloth-making

The climate of the country plays an important role in deciding the type of garments to be worn by the people suitable to its climatic conditions. Chamba as a whole has a cold to extremely cold climate and snowy winters. The higher peaks of its mountains remain mostly covered with thick layer of snow throughout the year. So

1. *Rajuḍ* is derived from a Sanskrit word *Rajju*, meaning a rope.
2. Bhupender Nath Datta, *Indian Art in Relation to Culture*, Calcutta (1978), pp. 69-70.

mostly its inhabitants wear woollen dresses throughout the year. The woollen cloth is known as *paṭṭu* in Chamba region. The *paṭṭu* is prepared from the wool obtainable from sheep. All the sheep who are to be sheared are given a bath. They are then let free to dry in the sun. When their fleece is completely dry, an elderly man catches hold of sheep one by one and shears the wool. The wool is then combed with both the hands, which practice in local dialect is called *fandhṇā* or *fanṇā*. From shearing of sheep to the last phase of preparing the final product *paṭṭu*, the entire job is done by hand. The wool is processed and refined and cleaned by thrashing with the help of carding bow called *panjaṇi*. The process is called *panjaṇā*. Thereafter, a crude thread is prepared through *charkhā* (spinning wheel). Later on this thread is further refined and made sturdy by twisting it around the wooden spindle whorls, *unshāṇ*. Now the thread is in its final form. Warp and woof are then ready to be weaved into a warm cloth *paṭṭu*, through a hand-loom, *rachh*. Finally the finished product is refined by a special washing process, *manḍṇā*.[1]

Most of the scholars believe that Aryans wore woollen clothes on the basis that there is frequent use of word *avi* for sheep and word *urṇa*[2] for wool in Vedic literature. It is also said that they used woollen cloth for the filtration of their much coveted godly drink known as *soma*. Terms used for all the varieties of woollen cloth in Buddhist literature is *kambalā*. In the pre-historic to first century B.C. linen was common though we do not know where it was manufactured. Blankets were also produced from a mixture of *kasumā* fibre and wool. Besides the above mentioned material for manufacturing dress, cloth was manufactured from hemp bark, *bhanga*, *kusā* grass, bark, wood, animal and human hairs and feathers etc. Skins of lions, tigers, leopards, cow and deer, etc.

1. Crushing and washing with feet in a big hole in a stone or in another identical *manḍni* prepared by a log of wood.
2. Lord Buddha is said to have a woollen mark on his forehead which is known as *urṇa*.

were also used for the purposes of beddings and clothes. In Chamba region the skins of rams and goats, etc. are still in use for some varieties of clothing and bedding.

6. Chamba Costumes: Historical Perspective

It cannot be said for certain, what was the dress of the inhabitants of Chamba region when Raja Maru travelling all the way from Kalāpa-grāma, set up the kingdom here in circa 500 A.D. If we are to go by the general trend of the dresses worn in India then it can be conjectured that both the males and females of Chamba walked bare breasted, although it is possible that because of the cold climate they must have wrapped their bodies with warm shawls (blankets) hung loosely over the shoulders. To cover the lower limbs they must have worn a loose *dhoti* gathered in front in the form of a fall between the legs and secured at the waist with some sort of waist band. The females probably wrapped a fine woollen blanket or *chaḍār* around their waist and gathered in front in the form of a fall. The living example of this is the *ḍoḍ* worn by the women of Churāh even today. To quote Charles Fabri:

> ". . . . It is much more likely that in northern India where the winter is and was harsh, men and women wore a thick material for a kind of a shawl and wrapped themselves up in it when the weather demanded."[1]

There used to be a custom in Chamba that during a special worship ceremony of Lord Śiva, known as *Nuwālā*, the *jogi* from a Natha sect, who presided over the ceremony, was presented with an unstitched garment *maikhal*, made of a cotton sheet, having a hole in the centre for head. This was worn by the *jogi* during the whole of the ceremony of *Nuwālā*. In the olden days the *maikhal* used to be made of a woollen blanket. To quote Bhupendra Nath Dutta:

---

1. Charles Louis Fabri, *Indian Dress—A Brief History*, New Delhi (1960), p. 22.

> ". . . . that the Hindu religious institution and rites still betray their chalcolithic trace as is seen in the injunction of the scriptures that the priest and the laymen should wear unsewn cloth during worship."[1]

It is possible that the early settlers of this region wore this kind of dress which was tied or girdled at the waist with a band or a *paṭkā*. A 7th century bronze image of a devotee with lamp was discovered at Chhatrari near Brahmour which is now preserved in Bhuri Singh Museum at Chamba. Here the man is seen wearing a short *dhoti* held at waist with a band and a dagger tucked in it. According to Dr. V.C. Ohri, this figure represents Gugga, the master sculptor who had cast the idols of Lakshna Devi at Brahmour and Shakti Devi at Chhatrari (7th century A.D.). These bronze images, however, show angular '*cholis*' worn by the deities. This perhaps was necessitated by the colder climate of the region. These bronze images though fashioned after the Gupta taste bear provincial influence, hence it is possible that the sewn garments were also known to the inhabitants of this remote region much earlier than in any other part of northern India. Kalhana in his *Rājtarangni* also mentions this type of '*choli*'. Another interesting image at Brahmour is that of Gaṇeśa (7th century A.D.) who is seen wearing a leather jacket (*Vyaghra Charmā*) hinting towards the imperatives of colder weather of the region.

Brahmour and Gaddis command an important position in the political and cultural history of Chamba. Brahmour was the capital of the state before Sahila Varman founded the new capital city of Chamba. It is possible that Sahila Varman at the time of migration from Brahmour to Chamba (10th century A.D.) was accompanied by a Gaddi army, although a majority of Gaddis must have liked to stay back in their ancestral land. Gaddis were known even in Panini's time (circa 5th century B.C.). He refers to them as Gabdik and their territory as Gabdīkā. In a way the dress of Gaddis still

1. Bhupendra Nath Dutta, *Indian Art in Relation to Culture*, Calcutta (1978), p. 98.

resembles the Indo-Scythian dresses as seen in some of the Kushan sculptures of Mathura of 2nd-4th century A.D. A fountain stone slab (10th century A.D.) discovered recently in the Naga shrine at Gum located half way between Chamba and Brahmour, shows an Indo-Scythian warrior drawing a bow. Scores of other fountain stone slabs from Churāh and Pāngi of 11th to 13th century A.D. depict figurines adorning costumes which faintly resemble Indo-Scythian dresses. This garb is worn by the donors and the donees of these commemorative slabs and their other associates, while the gods and other deities on the slabs are shown in their classical costumes. The outer walls of the temple of Lakshmi Narayan in Chamba (10th century A.D.) are replete with figures of musical instrumentalists in Indo-Scythian and local dresses, busy playing upon their respective instruments.

Although Chamba was never invaded by the Muslims but there was a series of immigration caused by the advancement of Ghaznavi forces into the Punjab plains. Since the immigrants belonged to the same cultural background, it can be conjectured that the dress habits of Chamba people might not have undergone any significant and serious change because of this influx of such refugees. The tradition of erection and dedication of fountain stone slabs continued in Chamba till 14th century A.D., but no figure cast on these slabs appears in distinctly Muslim dress, though a fountain stone slab depicting Mughal type '*jāmā*' is preserved in the Bhuri Singh Museum at Chamba. Already in Akbar's time Mughal costumes and textiles became known in Chamba and the Chamba treasury had until the great fire of 1937 A.D. preserved some beautiful pieces of Mughal Imperial costumes which were the presents of Emperor Jahangir to Princes Janardan and Bishamber of Chamba (1622 A.D). (It was first the rajas of Nurpur who introduced more of Mughal culture into the Beas valley).

It was during the Mughal period, especially in the reign of Shahjahan and Aurangzeb (1627-1707 A.D.) that men of upper classes all over northern India started wearing the type of dresses which were in vogue in the Mughal court, with some slight variations suitable to the local needs and conditions. In the vicinity of Chamba it were perhaps rajas of Nurpur who introduced Mughal culture to the Beas valley. Raja Prithvi Singh of Chamba (1641-1664 A.D.) was a contemporary of Shahjahan and a frequent visitor to his court. He was the first to introduce the Mughal style of court-life in Chamba also which was then prevalent amongst all the Rajput princes under Mughal influence. The wooden doors of state Kothi at Brahmour (now in Bhuri Singh Museum, Chamba) shows Raja Prithvi Singh and his courtiers in the Mughal costumes. This door belongs to Raja Umed Singh's period (1748-1764 A.D.).

The Chamba paintings are also very authentic and informative social documents of the history of those times. The study of these paintings reveal that while the men of those days wore Mughal style dresses of their times, the women-folk clung to their own traditional dresses except for Mughal '*peshwāj*', which was worn for going out of the house. The Pahāḍi paintings of the Sikh period show that the costumes of nobles in Chamba underwent a drastic change in the reign of Raja Charat Singh (1808-1844 A.D.) due to Sikh influence. Vigne, the European traveller, who visited Chamba during Raja Charat Singh's reign states that Jorawar Singh, the younger brother of Raja was very handsome and was always dressed in very dandy Sikh costume. The paintings preserved in Bhuri Singh Museum, Chamba, also show Raja Charat Singh dressed in Sikh fashion. Another painting shows Wazir Bagha in Sikh costume giving hearing to a Gaddi petitioner. The costume consisted of a flaring knee-length '*jāmā*', tight '*chuḍidār-pyjāmā*, '*kulhadār*' cap and untrimmed beared.

How far the present dress of Gaddis truly represents their ancient garb, is difficult to say for certain. Till the near future, however, a tradition continued to be adhered to. Whenever a new Raja ascended the throne of Chamba, at the time of consecration he was presented by the Gaddis of Brahmour a fine *paravā* (Gaddi costume) betokening that the Raja originally belonged to their tribe. The presentation of this dress was a mark of respect and loyalty of his ancient subjects. It is also believed that this garb is an attire of Lord Śiva. The Raja would wear this fine garb and hold a full *darbār* (court) in that attire.[1]

Raja would, however, do this only for a day. This old tradition continuing for centuries indicates that the founder of Brahmour, Raja Maru was a Gaddi and Brahmour itself was 'Gadarean', the seat par-excellence of Gaddi tribe. Regarding this garb having been associated with Lord Śiva, a legend is held popular in Chamba. Mr. R.C. Paul Singh writes:

> "According to the legend Jai Sthamba was the son of a ruling chief of some unnamed place in Rajputana and had fallen out with his father. He was turned out of the domain. Jai Sthamba decided to renounce the world and approached a holy man whom he accepted as his 'Guru'. The holy man advised him to lead the life of a Rajput and directed him towards this area where he could establish his principality. When he reached Kharamukh (a place near about Brahmour proper in Brahmour sub-division) with his followers, he was greeted by another saintly person named Agyachari Rishi. The Rishi had visited him at the dictates of Lord Śiva who had directed him in a dream to welcome the prince with the offering of a '*ṭopa*', a '*cholā*', and a '*ḍora*', the attire of the god. Anyhow, according to Chamba Vaṁśāvalī, the first prince who established his principality at Brahmour was Jai Sthamba, son of Maru."[2]

1. "The last Rajah before the Republic of India incorporated the state in the province of Himachal Pradesh was an enlightened ruler who undertook substantial public works so that the state became more administratively unified than at any previous time in its history. At his coronation, each of the nationalities in the state participated but on the first day the Rajah, dressed in the Gaddi uniform, was crowned as a 'Gaddi'. The Rajah and the Gaddis felt that a special relationship existed between them."

   William H. Newell, Report on Scheduled Castes and Scheduled Tribes, Census of India (1961), p. 5. (This report is on Brahmour).
2. R.C. Paul Singh, *A Village Survey—Brahmour* (1961), p. 5.

2

COSTUMES OF GADDIS

1. GADDIS

The origin of word *Gaddi* is somewhat uncertain. Great grammarian Panini (5th century B.C.) named present day Brahmour as Gabdīkā, and their residents as Gabdīk.[1] The word *Gaddi*, therefore, is considered to be a corrupt derivative of Gabdīk. Dr. Hazari Prasad Dwivedi was emphatic in his belief that the word *Gaddi* originated from *Gāḍar*, meaning a sheep,[2] a herd of sheep, or a string made of intestines of a sheep used in a musical instrument.[3] The word *Gāḍri* or *Gaḍariya* is used in almost all the north Indian languages for a person who tends the herd of sheep and goat. So the original *Gāḍri* (a person engaged in tending to the herd of sheep) could have evolved as such—*Gāḍar-Gāḍari—Gaḍrī-Gaḍḍī—Gaddi* (गाडर, गाडरी, गड़री, गड्डी, गददी) in the course of time. This etymology tends to underline the main profession of Gaddis as the herdsmen. It is also surmised that the word was derived from Gāhar, an alpine pasture where Gaddis graze their herds of sheep.

Gaddis traditionally believe that they migrated to Brahmour from the plains. According to a popular tradition, the Chauhan Rajput Gaddis and Brahmin Gaddis accompanied Raja Ajaya Verman to Brahmour in Chamba in circa A.D. 760-780, while the

---

1. Vasudev Sharan Aggarwal, *Panini-Kaleen Bharatvarsha*, Banaras (2012 Vik.), pp. 43 and 76.
2. Bṛht Hindi Kosh, Varanasi: Gyan Mandal, 4th Ed., 2030 Vik.
3. Bāj Surāg Ki Gāḍar Tanti (बाज सुराग कि गाडर तांती) *Ramcharitmānas*.

Khatri Gaddis seem to have fled to Brahmour to escape persecution at the hands of Aurangzeb. Some scholars believe that the majority of Brahmins migrated to Brahmour during the reign of King Maru Varman (circa 680-760 A.D.). It is believed that the Rajputs came to Brahmour as soldiers initially with the Brahmour prince, Raja Jai Sthamba. During the Muslim period a large body of Khatris is believed to have migrated to these hills from Lahore. It was much later that these immigrants started having matrimonial relations with the Rajput Gaddis. Popular belief of Gaddi migration is well-fortified by the fact that almost all important Brahmin, Rajput and Khatri *gotras* are extant and prevalent among the Gaddis of Brahmour.

General Cunningham was inclined to identify the Gaddis with the ancient Ghandaridav or Gangaridae. He was of the view that the ancient name of Brahmour was Varmanpura. Hermann Goetz opines:

> "The Gaddis (Gadhaiyas) were a semi-nomadic tribe inhabiting the Punjab probably the Takkādeśa, though originally they may have come from Hindukush region, as they have affinities with Kafirs. Whether the early advance of Sāhis or the Muslim invasion had driven them into Kangra valley we do not know for certain."[1]

He further mentions that Gaddis may not have migrated before 10th century A.D. to Brahmour.[2] This view of Hermann Goetz also finds confirmation from the fact that the generic name of Gaddis includes only Brahmins, Rajputs, Khatris and Rathis, and not the classes known as Sipis, Bāḍhis, Rehāḍas, Lohārs and Hālis which have also been residing in Brahmour from a very early period, but outside Brahmour they generally style themselves as Gaddis. This clearly indicates that Gaddis do not constitute the main strata or the total of population of Brahmour. Some historians who maintain

1. Harmann Goetz, *Early Wooden Temples of Chamba*, Netherlands (1955), p. 34.
2. Ibid., p. 25.

that the original home of Gaddis was Buddhal valley (Brahmour) in Chamba, substantiate their claim from the chronicles of Kulu state, wherein it is mentioned that a certain Gaddi army had attacked Kulu state in 10th century A.D. during the reign of Raja Narad Pala of Kulu. The place where the army encamped is still popularly known as Gaddi-padar (Gaddi-plain).

2. The Land of Gaddis

The popular belief of migration of Gaddis apart, any and every Gaddi believes Brahmour to be his original homeland. Today Gaddis have spread to almost all areas of Chamba district, particularly Chamba and Bhaṭṭiyāt tehsils, besides the neighbouring districts of Kangra and Lahul and Spiti in Himachal, and Gurdaspur in Punjab. But any Gaddi remembers and mentions with pride that his original place has been Brahmour. Panini had named Brahmour as Gabdīkā and its residents as Gabdīk, Gaddi being a corrupt derivative. Panini referred to Trigarta as a confederation (*Sangha*) of six divisions called as 'Trigarta-Shashṭh'. These six constituents of the confederacy were Kauṇḍopartha, Dāṇḍaki, Krausṭakī, Jālamāni, Brāhmgupta and Jānaki.[1] Dr. V.S. Aggarwal identified the above Brāhmgupta with present Brahmour.[2] Brāhmgupta has also been identified with the Bharmaras of *Purāṇas*.[3] It is also believed that it may be the same Brahmpura as enlisted in the *Bṛhātsaṁhitā*.[4]

3. Gaddi Way of Life

As compared to the other tribes of India, Gaddis live well and enjoy outdoor life. There is no polyandry prevalent amongst them and they rigidly follow the Hindu way of life. The Gaddis of

1. Vasudev Sharan Aggarwal, *Panini-Kaleen Bharatvarsha*, Banaras (2012 Vik.), pp. 43 & 76.
2. Ibid., p. 458.
3. Tej Ram Sharma, 'Ancient Tribes of Himachal Pradesh' in *Himachal Art and Archaeology*, edited by V.C. Ohri, State Museum, Shimla (1980), p. 64.
4. Ibid., p. 64.

Brahmour pass their summers at Brahmour tending to their cattle and land. The Gaddi women look after the household affairs. With the onset of winter, life at such a high altitude becomes difficult. In the knee-deep snow no provision for man or beast is possible. The Gaddis, therefore, lock their homes and move down the Ravi valley in search of new pastures. Mostly Gaddis move to the Kangra valley, lower areas in Chamba and particularly to Chamba town where they spend their winters. Sometimes, some of their women-folk are employed as maid-servants by the town people, and the men usually look after their sheep, work on the roads or pick up any odd job available. But no Gaddi will do the work of a menial, a cobbler, a sweeper or a butcher.

Even today the Gaddis call Kangra and its adjoining parts by the ancient name Jandhar (Jallandhar). This indicates that the Gaddis had a very old tradition of migration to the lower lands in winter. A Gaddi while travelling with his flock of sheep is invariably accompanied by a fierce looking dog, which over-jealously guards the moving wealth, *dhan*, i.e. the herd of sheep of his master and maintains discipline amongst the sheep by his occasional growls. The special breed of dog goes by the name of '*Gaddā-Kuttā*' or Gaddi-dog. This dog is very dear to the Gaddis. The Gaddi woman or Gaddan, like a loyal and dutiful housewife, always accompanies her husband in his travels. A Gaddi couple journeying on the road surrounded by their herds of sheep presents an ever delightful picture. The Gaddis worship Śiva as their principal deity and probably it was for this reason that they selected Brahmour, a place not far away from mount Kailash, the abode of Lord Śiva. The commanding temple of Mani-Mahesh at Brahmour and Śiva temple at Harsar confirm the above view. They affectionately call their land as the place of Śiva or Śiv-Bhumi. They have firmly believed that their destiny is guided by Lord Śiva. They speak the western Pahāḍi dialects, known as Gādī or Bharmouri (Brahmouri) in Chamba.

Although the original homeland of the Gaddis remains

Brahmour, Gaddis now inhabit the areas of Chamba, Bhaṭṭiyāt, and Churāh tehsils as well. The population of Brahmour presents a fusion of may races.

4. Costumes of Gaddis (men)

4.1. Ṭop and Sāfā (Head-dress)

The Gaddi costumes for men and women are very conspicuous and esoteric. The woollen *ṭop* (old head-dress) of the men is of a peculiar shape. It has a flap and a peak-like formation, which Gaddis presume to represent the mountain Kailash of Lord Śiva. The Gaddi usually keep the flap folded up during the ordinary weather but it is pulled down over the ears and neck in times of severe cold or when there is a mourning in the family. The Gaddi is fond of decorating his *ṭop* (peak-cap) with a *kalgi* (tuft of feathers) of bird *nilgar* (*monal*—Eng. Impeyan pheasant). The *ṭop* is also often adorned with dry flowers or beads. A red handkerchief is also pinned at the top of the cap, so that during dance, when Gaddi takes a swing, the red handkerchief unfurls in the air giving a very colourful effect to the whole dance sequence. This sort of head-dress is falling in disuse for ordinary wear and the Gaddis now usually keep this head-dress for special occasions, such as, ceremonies, fairs and festivals and choral dances. Ordinary head-dress of Gaddis for daily use consists of a *sāfā* or *pagḍi* (turban), which is a long sheet of cloth tied around the head by giving it numerous folds. The *sāfā* is coloured according to the fancy of Gaddi. Mention may also be made to peculiar type of head-dress known as *kanṭop*. In Chameālī dialects it is also called '*kanḍhapu-ṭopi*'. The peculiar feature of this kind of head-dress is that the wearer can cover his ears and neck in the severe cold. Sometimes it is also embroidered.

An ancient tradition of Gaddis which holds true till present times is that it is considered disrespectful to move about in the society with an uncovered head. The *sāfā* is a symbol of respect and dignity. A saying which is still popular amongst the Gaddis and is invoked with some kind of humour by the town people reads like this:

> '*nang serai kuhāḍ bajai, ḍhak serai permaisrā*'
> (नंग सिरे कुहाड़ बजे, ढ़क सिरे परमेसरा)

It means that an axe falls on the bare head. May the head of everybody be covered by the grace of God.

Gaddis also wear a woollen *ṭopi* (cap) which may slightly be embroidered with coloured woollen threads.

4.2. Cholā, Choli, Khaptān (Kaftān)

(a) Cholā

On the body proper a *paṭṭu* gown called *cholā* is worn, which reaches just below the knees. It is made of whitish woollen cloth and acquires a greyish-brown tinge with the lapse of time. This gown has full sleeves, deep collars and is closed crosswise over the breasts and is gathered round the waist by a *ḍorā* or a long black woollen rope worn in many folds. The *cholā* is thus loose above the *ḍorā* and the receptacle thus formed is called *kokh*. The Gaddis carry many of their belongings in this *kokh*. It takes 18 to 23 metres of *paṭṭu* to make a *cholā*. The *cholā* is a Sanskrit word designating body as well as a sewn garment. The *cholā* opens up and unfurls like a full bloomed flower from below when a Gaddi takes a swing while dancing in the company of his kins-folk. The borders, back and the shoulders of the *cholā* are embroidered with white and red woollen threads. Another *cholā* (gown for body proper) is made of heavy rough cloth and is worn by *puhālas* (shepherds) during their rough and tough professional callings.

(b) Choli

It is made of light fine cloth and sometimes embroidered with white woollen thread. It is worn by Gaddis on special occasions. In all other respects *choli* is similar to *cholā*, the only point of difference being the quality of cloth.

(c) Khaptān

Khaptān is prepared from the *paṭṭu* of superior quality, and is soft to touch and light to wear. It is embroidered with white and red woollen thread at the neck and around the shoulders. It has no collars and is worn by Gaddi dignitaries on special occasions. It is, however, falling into disuse now.

On the occasion of a dance Gaddis fold a red or some other gaudy coloured scarf in triangular shape and pin it upon the back side between their shoulder in such a way that apex of the triangle points downwards. There is also a myth prevalent amongst Gaddis that the red coloured scarf wards off evil spirits and dreaded diseases. A long *paṭkā* is hung around the neck and the two ends of *paṭkā* are made to pass through the *ḍorā*.

4.3. Ḍorā or Gātri

The long rope made of wool, fastened around the waist in many folds by both male and female Gaddis is called *ḍorā* or *gātri*. It is probably meant for giving support to the waist while climbing. The woollen *ḍorā* has also the utility of keeping them warm apart from serving the purpose of a felt belt. It is a popular belief among the Gaddis that so long the rope is tied on their waist, their wealth and their sheep will also be bound up and remain with them. Some anthropologists suggest that Gaddis have to travel long and high along with their sheep in search of fresh pastures, and the long rope tied to their waist comes in handy for a good number of chores. The *ḍorā* also serves the purpose of rope if there is no ordinary rope available. Gaddis are so habitual of wearing this *ḍorā* that they are likely to suffer from cramps in the stomach if they don't wear it. A Gaddi is sentimental about his *ḍorā* and calls it *Śiva-ri-seli*, meaning thereby that it is the auspicious symbol of Śiva, and they wear it in his name. *Seli*[1] is a symbolic Śiva-rope worn by Nāth Jogis all over northern India for centuries. The *ḍorā* can also be used for tying the baggage while on move. The *ḍorā* keeps the Gaddi watchful and alert which are the necessary conditions for keeping watch and ward over the sheep grazing in open pastures.

Another name of *ḍorā* is *gātri. Gātri* is derived from a Sanskrit word *gātar*, designating human body. When a Gaddi has to spend nights in the open pastureland, he takes off his *cholā*, and spreads it on the ground to serve as a bed sheet while his *ḍorā* serves the purpose of a pillow. Then he lies down taking the name of Śiva and the hard days work makes him fall asleep instantly. Before falling asleep if he is in company, there may be a small chit-chat over the smoking-rounds on his *nerelā* (*hukkā*). Even a Gaddi kid is not spared of the *ḍorā*. The *ḍorā* is usually of black colour and is made of two *aṭṭis* (hangs). Each *aṭṭi* has a length of 12-20 hands for Gaddans (female) and 20 to 25 hands for Gaddis (male). It varies from 40 to 60 yards in length, and weighs about 2 to 3 kilograms.

The special kind of *ḍorā* is decorated with buttons of *sipi* (sea-shell), *moti* (white pearls) and *chaiṇian* (चैनंए) (rice grains) and *baṭṭu* (black beads). The entire mass of *ḍorā* is tied with a red and white thread at intervals. The purpose is purely decorative. From this *ḍorā* hang a few decorative pieces, *baglu* and *bagli*. *Baglu* is a leather pouch made of goat or sheep skin, decorated with beads called *ratties*. With this *baglu* is attached a *sangli* (iron chain), from which hang some other accessories like a knife and an appliance known as *ruṇkā* (flint-lock) for starting fire. Along with tobacco the *baglu* also contains a cotton-like substance *bhujlu*, which is obtained after processing some kind of wild leaves which catch fire easily. Gaddis in order to make fire strike *ruṇkā* against *sukrāh* (a kind of white flint stone) held in his other hand along with

1. The Sanskrit dictionary defines *Seli* as plaited band of cotton used by 'Yogis'.

bhujlu. The sparks thus produced are caught by *bhujlu* and the fire is made. Gaddis are fond of playing upon flute, and this they keep tucked in the *ḍorā.*

4.4. Woollen Suthan (Pyjāmā)

We do not find trousers mentioned in Vedas.[1] The Gaddis also prefer to walk bare-legged. They may, however, wear woollen *pyjāmā* loose to the knees but fitting tight at the lower part of the leg and ankle, where it is made to rest. Some also wear now cotton (*khaddar*) *pyjāmā*[2] called '*chuḍidār suthan*'.[3]

4.5. Kurtā

It is also prepared from woollen hand-made cloth known as *paṭṭu.* It is also called '*kameej*' (shirt) and may be stitched from cotton cloth like any ordinary shirt of today.

4.6. Footwear

(a) Juṭṭā

The footwear of Gaddis consists of an open shoe or a *juṭṭā.* It is made of crude leather and is sturdy enough for undertaking rugged journeys. They also wear Chamba chappals. The Gaddis usually remain bare-footed, but now with the advent of plastic footwear

---

1. ". . . . . of course it may be regarded that the wearing of trousers was an innovation of the northern invaders. We have already said that trousers had been unknown in the sub-tropical and tropical parts of Asia, hence it cannot be a wonder that it had been unknown in the Vedic and post-Vedic India. Trousers were unknown in Achamenid-Persia. The Persians borrowed it from the northern Medes. The Arabs of the Abbasid period borrowed it from the Persians." Bhupendra Nath Dutta, *Indian Art in Relation to Culture,* Calcutta (1978), p. 70.
2. Pājāmā is the Persian word: 'Pā' means foot or leg; jāmā means costume, i.e. the costume for leg.
3. "सुत्थन या पायजामा शकों की पोशाक थी, जो उन्ही के साथ ईसापूर्व और पश्चात की प्रथम शताब्दियों में भारत आयी। पीछे हमारे राजाओं ने उसे अपनी पोशाक में दाखिल कर लिया, यह अपने सिक्कों पर सुत्थन पहने गुप्त राजाओं को देखने से मालूम होता है . . . ." ऋग्वेदिक आर्य, इलाहाबाद (1957), p. 157.

which has flooded the market, the Gaddis now no longer travel bare-footed.

(b) Jaḍulā

Jaḍulā are made of rough goat-hairs and are used for crossing the heavy snowy passes during winter. They resemble gum-boots or long boots.

5. Costumes of Gaddans (women)

The dress of Gaddi women is feminine, bewitching and such that it enhances the beauty of a Gaddan. The dress proper i.e. *cholā* is the same as that worn by a Gaddi except that now the gown reaches down upto the ankles to cover the shapely legs of the Gaddan. The *cholā* of a Gaddi is now called *cholu* or *choli*. It is this similarity of dress between Gaddi and Gaddan that they make a striking pair. The Gaddis are of the belief that they assumed the garb of Śiva and Parvati, when they settled in Brahmour which they call 'Śiva-Bhumi' or Śiva-Land.

5.1. Ghunḍu (Head-dress)

The word *ghunḍ* or *jhunḍ* means a veil, and seems to be derivative of *ghungaṭ*. It appears that the tradition of *ghunḍu* amongst Gaddi women started with Muslim excursion into the hills or as a result of interaction with the higher classes of Hindus from plains who had already come in contact with Muslims. Earlier Hindu women never covered their faces. *Ghunḍu* is nothing else but a *dupaṭṭā*. The Gaddi women cover their head with the *ghunḍu* and then throw it around their shoulders. This head-dress may either be made of cotton or silk, and it comes in various shapes. The Gaddi women on special occasions like marriages and *Jātras* adorn themselves with colourful *dupaṭṭās* with *goṭṭā* work done on them. This kind of *dupaṭṭā* is called *dhankāwālā* or *goṭṭaiwālā ghunḍu*. The other kind of *dupaṭṭā* which is also worn on these occasions is named a *goṭhṇiwālā ghunḍu*. The main characteristic of this kind of *dupaṭṭā* is that a border of different coloured cloth is stitched on all the four sides of it. The length of the *ghunḍu* is usually 2.50 to 2.75 metres. For daily use the Gaddi women prefer to buy an ordinary *dupaṭṭā* from the market. *Dupaṭṭā* in local dialect (Brahmouri) is also called *chadru*.

5.2. Choli, Cholu and Luanchḍi

It will be appropriate here to differentiate between *choli, cholu* and *luanchḍi*. *Choli* is made out of the finest *paṭṭu*. It is a full sleeve dress, reaches upto ankels, and is reserved for special occasions. But *cholu* is used for daily wear in winter and is made of ordinary quality of *paṭṭu*. *Luanchḍi* is a light stuff made of chintz (pintadoes). It is a sleeveless garb but resembles *cholu* in all other respects. It is similar to *peshwāj* but lighter to wear. It takes about 12 to 20 metres of cloth to make a complete *luanchḍi*, but now-a-days it is generally made from 10 to 14 metres of cloth. In short, *luanchḍi* may be called a cotton gown worn in the same way as the *cholu*. A sleeveless vest is attached to the pleated portion to make a *luanchḍi* and *choli* or *cholu*. The front portion of the vest of *luanchḍi* is decorated with frills and *goṭṭā*. The *cholā* as a sewn garment of women is mentioned in an ancient text *Amarkosha* (4th-6th century A.D.).

5.3. Ḍorā or Gātri

The *choli, cholu* and *luanchḍi* is held together at the waist by a *ḍorā*. This is the same as that used by the Gaddi men and serves the same functions.

Special mention may be made of the decorative piece called '*chhaṭṭā*', which Gaddi women hang from their *ḍorās*. The *chhaṭṭā* consists of a rounded mirror fixed on a small circular piece made of goat or sheep's skin, and decorated all around with red beads called *ratties* and read thread.

5.4. Kameej

Underneath the *cholu* the Gaddi women wear a simple shirt, with a half belt in the front. The shirt is similar to the one worn by the men-folk now-a-days, except for a slight difference in the fall.

5.5. Suthan Chuḍidār

The Gaddi women prefer to keep their legs bare underneath the *cholu*, but sometimes a tight *chuḍidār* cotton *suthan* (pair of trousers) may be worn. The *chuḍidār suthan* becomes all the more a necessity while dancing for, the gown tends to fly high while taking a swing. The old Gaddi women of upper classes prefer to wear a *paṭṭu suthan. Shalwār* is now becoming a common wear among Gaddans.

5.6. Mochḍu or Mochḍi (Footwear)

The word *mochḍu* or *mochḍi* is derived from *mochi*, which means cobbler. *Mochḍu* hence becomes a product of a *mochi. Mochḍu* or *mochḍi* is nothing but a *juṭṭā* or *juṭṭi* (shoes) decorated with *tillā* work. Chamba *chappal* is also common with both female and male Gaddis these days.

3

COSTUMES OF GUJJARS

1. GUJJARS

There are various views regarding the origin of Gujjar tribe. The word Gujjar is derived from the name Gurjara, which became common in India in 7th century A.D., but went out of use in 8th century A.D.[1] The Gurjaras first appeared in the Indian history after the fall of Gupta empire (6th century A.D.). They seem to have been dragged into India by the white Huna invasion. From the study of ancient Indian history it appears that the name Gurjara did not refer to a particular tribe or people but was collective appellation of various tribes of various origins. These Gurjaras became Hindu and established many Rajput kingdoms in northern India. The upper Gurjara class was merged into Rajputs leaving it to their nomadic brethern to preserve their identity. However, it may be pointed out that most of those still calling themselves Gujjars in the Himalaya are Muslim immigrants from the plains known as 'Sunis'. Originally they were Hindus, but seem to have embraced Islam during the reign of Aurangzeb.

According to Sir A. Cunningham the homeland of Gujjars is Gujarat which existed even before the birth of Christ.[2] Certain unforeseen circumstances made them to migrate from Gujarat-Kathiawar to Jammu and Kashmir, and later to Himachal Pradesh.[3]

1. Hermann Goetz, *Early Wooden Temples of Chamba*, Netherlands (1955), p. 42.
2. Thakur Sen Negi, *Scheduled Tribes of Himachal Pradesh: A Profile*, Meerut (1976), p. 116.
3. Ibid., p. 116.

There are many localities and regions called after Gurjaras. Gujranwala, Gujarat and Gujjar Khan (in west Punjab) are associated with these people. According to certain historians, Gurjaras had migrated from Georgia, a former republic of the U.S.S.R. Georgia is known in Persia as Gurjarastan. A study of the Gujjars in 1967 A.D. by Prof. Georgi Chogoshvili of the Georgian Academy of Science, pointed out striking similarities between the Georgians and Gujjars. K.M. Munshi points towards the Indian origin of Gujjars. The name Gujjar first appears in the Indian literature in 7th century A.D. in the *Harash Charitra* of Ban Bhat. Hiuen Tsang also mentions them. In Sanskrit the word Gurjar was used, and now-a-days Gujjar is used in place of Gurjar which predicts the qualities of a warrior community.

Pratihār Gujjars and most of others also believe to have descended from Suryavaṁśi Kshatriyas and connect themselves with Shri Ram Chandra. There is also another view in this connection that in Ujjain Rajputs performed a big '*Yajna*' and some Gujjar Rajas accepted to act as *Pratihārs* (protectors) of this '*Yajna*'.

According to some scholars Gujjars belong to the ancient clan of 'Groter-Kshatriyas', who were brave men. These people enjoyed the title of *Gorjan*, which meant leader of the masses. According to a well-known legend the Kshatriya clan was destroyed twenty one times by Parsuram. Brahmins fearing the total extinction of Kshatriyas from the face of the earth, performed a '*Yajna*' on the peak of Mount Abu and a new Kshatriya community named as Gurjar or Gujjar was born from the holy fire.

2. Chamba Gujjars

According to a local legend, Gujjars were allowed to enter the erstwhile state of Chamba as a reward for old Gujjar woman who had served the life of a close relative of the ruling prince of Chamba of that time. Another legend tells about some Gujjars being invited by the queen of Chamba about 300-350 years ago for the supply of milk for the royal family and people.

The Gujjars of Chamba today are mostly pastoral and live a purely nomadic life. They wander throughout the year in search of new pastures for their buffalloes and cows. Unlike Gaddis who move with their flocks of sheep and goats along with the members of their family, Gujjars move in caravans. In summer, they move with their families and cattle to the higher regions in search of new pastures and in winter they move down to the plains of Punjab. They live in a joint-family and are monogamous. Transhumance based on buffaloes is the central feature of Gujjar culture. Whole of their economy rests on milk which is always in demand and even becomes a rare commodity at times. The Gujjars began to use summer pastures only about the mid-19th century A.D.[1] Possibly, changed political conditions forced them to seek new grazing lands at that time. The Gujjars are accustomed to walking long distances and think little of going 8 or 10 miles to visit a friend, but now with the opening up of transport facilities, a Gujjar would also like to have a bus ride like any one else even for a short distance. With their *hinā*-coloured trimmed beard and tall and hefty figure they give the impression of Mughal nobles. Because of their conspicuous dress, they can be recognised from a long distance. Inspite of their awe-inspiring personality they are peace-loving people, and proud of their traditional way of life. It is never heard of a Gujjar walking out of his closely-knit community and accepting any other way of life.

A Gujjar of today would like to have small land which he could call his own and live on agriculture. He is gradually trying to shed his nomadic character. To avail himself of the modern amenities he loves to lead a stable life. The modern ways of life are certainly going to affect him and the day does not seem to be faraway, when the Gujjar tribe will merge completely with local rural and the town-folk and may be heard or seen of no more in their present form.

1. Thakur Sen Negi, *District Gazetteer of Chamba* (1963), p. 344.

Linguistically, 'Gujjari' the language of Gujjars is only slightly different from western Pahāḍi dialect prevalent in this area. Both the *Bhārata Nāṭya Śāstra* and Varāhamihira observed that the Khāśas adopted the 'Bahlika' language, which in this case can mean only 'Gujjari', as the Gurjaras are believed to have come from Central Asia.[1] The 'Gujjari' is akin to Rajasthani (Mewari and Mewati). Now Gujjars inhabit, more or less, the entire district of Chamba.

3. Costumes of Gujjars (Men)

The costumes of Gujjars present a fascinating study. It is not certain how far the present costumes represent the original garb worn by Gujjars. Unlike Gaddis the Gujjars wear dresses made of simple cotton cloth, purchased ready from the market. The colours which they choose may be either blue, red or black. A Gujjar will not wear clothes made of any other colour. The colours are dark and gaudy and juxtaposed to each other. Hence, a Gujjar is easily recognisable from a distance because of the peculiarity of his dress. There are few shops in Chamba district, which cater to the needs of clothes of Gujjars with specific colours, textures, patterns and designs. Similarly there are only a few tailors who specialise in stitching specific Gujjar attire.

3.1. Sāfā

A Gujjar adorns a turban on his head vaguely resembling Mughal head-dress. His *hinā*-dyed and trimmed beard alongwith his head-gear in Mughal style gives the expression of a noble coming right out of the Mughal court. The turban is made of simple, white muslin cloth, and is 3.65 to 5.50 metres in length. Gujjar children wear a Gujjari *ṭopi* akin to a *kanṭop*, having peaked top made from cotton cloth of different colours.

---

1. Hermann Goetz, *Early Wooden Temples of Chamba*, Netherlands (1955), p. 12.

3.2. Bangāli Kameej or Kalidār Kurtā

A Gujjar wears a long and loose shirt which comes up to his knees. The *kameej* as it is known is invariably of blue and black colour, but he may wear stark white shirt also sometimes.

The *kameej* is of two types, *Bangāli* or *Kalidār*. The Bangāli *kameej* is worn by the young generation, while the old and middle aged prefer *kalidār kurtā. Kalidār kurtā* is similar to 'Lacknavi *kurtā*', except that it has collars and cuffs. *Bangāli kameej* is like the one worn by Pathans, which reaches upto knees having collars and cuffs. Both the shirts have buttons and have pockets on one side.

3.3. Bāsket

Over the shirt a vest-coat is worn, which is invariably of black colour. It is decorated with beads and buttons. It has two side-pockets which have frills. The frill is also used on the side and back of the vest-coat. It is of the same pattern as that worn by Jāts of Punjab.

3.4. Themat, Ghuṭanā, Silwār (Shalwār)

The Gujjars cover the lower limbs of their body by *themat, ghuṭanā* or *shalwār. Themat (lungi)* is unstitched piece of cloth of gaudy colour, and check-patterned. It is simply tied on the waist without the help of a string or a belt. In winter season it becomes difficult for a Gujjar to pull on with a simple *themat*. He is then seen wearing a simple cotton or woollen *ghuṭanā (chuḍidār pyjāmā)*. It is a baggy type[1] of dress loose at the thighs and knees, but fitting tight at the calf and ankels where it rests in numerous folds. The Gujjars on some occasion also wear *shalwār*. Now-a-days the Gujjars may be seen wearing a *pyjāmā* also.

---

1. "In the sixth century some Arab traveller described the King of Sindh as wearing baggy trousers." Bhupendra Nath Dutta, *Indian Art in Relation to Culture*, Calcutta (1978), p. 81.

3.5. Poti, Khaisi (Chāddar)

The Gujjars wrap a *chāddar* around their shoulders. It serves the same function as a shawl. This *chāddar* is of two kinds, *poti* or *khaisi*. *Poti* is meant to be used on special occasions, while *khaisi* is for the ordinary wear. Poti is generally 9 metres in length and is of white colour. *Khaisi* is roughly 4.50 metres in length and is of chequered pattern.

4. Costumes of Gujjaris (women)

A Gujjari is a beauty in her own right. The colourful costumes enhance the charm of her well-built body.

4.1. Joji (Head-dress) and Jhoomb

The credit for beautifying the head and face of a Gujjari goes to a caption-like object worn over her head which goes by the name of *joji* or *ṭopi*. *Joji* is like a bowl turned upside down over the head. It is made of cloth. With *joji* a cloth plait is attached which is made to hang in various longitudinal pleats over the back side. This cloth hangs upto the waist. *Joji* is usually stitched in criss-cross fashion with coloured threads.

Jhoomb is a type of head-gear made out of cotton sheet wrapped in a particular scarf-like manner. It is meant to protect the wearer from sun and rain.

4.2. Kurtā Kalidār

Gujjaris usually wear a loose *kalidār* black *kurtā* upto their knees. This *kurtā* is decorated with stitches of colourful threads done in criss-cross fashion and bears frill on the sides, cuffs and collars. Over the *kurtā* is worn vest-coat like that of Gujjar men-folk.

4.3. Salārā and Neelak

A Gujjari also wraps a *chāddar* (ṣheet) around her head and upper portion of her body. The *chāddar* is named as *salārā* and *neelak*. *Salārā* is 7 metres in length, while the length of a *neelak* comes to 9 metres. This *chāddar* is usually of dark colour bearing a red coloured strip for border all around.

4.4. Suthan Chuḍidār

The Gujjari women wear *suthan chuḍidār* in Jammu style to cover their legs. The *chuḍidār suthan* is tight upto ankles but loose at the thighs. The *suthan* is made out of a special kind of cloth called *susi*. *Susi* cloth is of back colour with red strips. Gujjaris now have also started wearing *shalwārs*.

4.5. Footwears

Desi Jüṭṭā is worn by both the male and female Gujjars.

4

COSTUMES OF PANGWĀLĀS

1. PANGWĀLĀS

Pāngi valley is situated in the middle Himalayan range, its altitude extending between 8,000 and 21,000 feet above the sea level. Two snowy ranges of Pir Panjāl (Pir-Pentsal) and Zaskar (Zanskar) enclose the valley rendering it completely isolated and difficult for access.

Pangwālā is a generic name for the inhabitants of Pāngi tehsil of Chamba. According to Hermann Goetz:

> "The real remnants of the old Gurjara kingdom must be sought in areas, which were not centres of political power and the population structure of which has since then been hardly disturbed, i.e. Churāh and Pāngi in the west, and Simla hills in the east."[1]

There is no doubt that the seat of Gurjara power was at Brahmour. But we have to look to the opposite direction towards Churāh and Pāngi for the remnants of Gurjara civilisation, as these territories remained comparatively free from foreign intervention. The population of Brahmour, however, presents a fusion of many races due to its reasonably mobile circumstances.

According to a common belief the settlers of Lahul and lower

1. Hermann Goetz, *Early Wooden Temples of Chamba*, Netherlands (1955), p. 44.

Chenab valley migrated to Pāngi in search of good lands and green pasture.

Another view holds that Rajput nobles sent their families to far away places like Pāngi to save them from molestation at the hands of Muslims. The Rajput nobles, thus free from the worry of their families, fought pitched battles with the Mughals and laid down their lives fighting. The Rajput families which were left behind by them at Pāngi, ultimately settled there for good.

The fountain stone slabs of Churāh and Pāngi are decorated with motifs, which without any doubt are taken from contemporary Hindu art, though the barbarian styles and trends point unmistakably to the Central Asian influence. Thus, it may be appropriate to conclude that the majority of the population migrated to Pāngi from Central Asia. The ancient name of Pāngi seems to be Pāngaṭi. The people of Pāngi have primitive social, religious and economic standards and follow a semi-nomadic way of life. The people depend mainly upon agriculture and cottage industry. Their hand-woven blankets and *thobis* (goat-hair carpets) sell out at good price.

The Pangwālās have no tradition of migration during winter, and they stay at home during all seasons of the year. The winter in Pāngi is long and severe. The Pangwālās take the help of wine, which is locally distilled from foodgrains, fruits and *guḍ* (jaggery) to ward off cold and boredom of the long wintery evenings. At the onset of winter the entire family moves down to spend the winter in a closed room in the basement of the house. There is sufficient warmth because of the kitchen, cattle and all the members of a family living together in one room.

The path to Pāngi leads through difficult mountain terrain and mountain passes which are at the high altitude of about 15,000 feet. In winter these passes become inaccessible to human approach and, as a result, the entire Pāngi area is isolated and cut-off from the rest of the world.

A typical constituent of the people of Pāngi are 'Bhoṭs', who are Buddhists. Many Buddhist shrines or Bhoṭories are also found in this area. The places where Bhoṭs live are called Bhoṭories.

Pangwālās are also sub-divided into high and low castes. The Halis, Lohārs, Meghs and Ḍāgis come from lower castes. Pangwālās speak Pangwāli dialect with many words common to Sanskrit. Bhoṭs, however, speak Bhoṭiā, a dialect distinct from Pangwāli.

2. Costumes of Pangwālās (men)

The Pangwālā dress has its own peculiar characteristics, suitable to the demands of extremely cold climate. The dress is made of both wool and cotton.

2.1. Ṭop or Ṭopi

The *ṭopi* of a Pangwālā is a simple white skull cap, with a flap at the back which is turned upwards. The *ṭopi* is generally piped at the lower end with a red or green cloth.

2.2. Kamari (Kameej)

The shirt of a Pangwālā is *kamari* meaning the one that is worn over his waist (*kamar*). This shirt is either woollen or cotton. The shirt is worn loose and terminates at the knees. Underneath this shirt, no under-garment is worn. The *kamari* (woollen shirt) has no collars and cuffs.

2.3. Chālaṇ[1] (Chuḍidār Pyjāmā)

Chalaṇā in Chameālī dialect means an act of walking. Since it is with the legs that one walks, hence the garment worn over the lower limbs is named by Pangwālās as *chālaṇ*. The *chālaṇ* in short

1. ". . . . the Sanskrit name for trousers is given as 'Chalana'. That name is still known in Indonesia. But the writer has not been able to discover the name in the Sanskrit texts . . . ." Bhupendra Nath Dutta, *Indian Art in Relation to Culture*, Calcutta (1978), p. 70.

is a *pyjāmā chuḍidār* or an ordinary *pyjāmā* worn loose upto the knees but tight below, with puckers at the calf and ankles. The *chālaṇ* is either a woollen or a cotton garment. It is also pronounced as '*chālar*'.

2.4. Koth (Coat) and Chogā

It is a long coat worn over the shirt and comes in many styles. This coat out-runs the shirt in length. Some Pangwālās are also seen wearing Gaddi-like *cholā*, which they term as *chogā*. Pangwālās who are a little ahead of their times adorn a modern European-cut coat also. The *koṭh* (coat) is tied-up at the waist with *mājhin* designating black and dark pink coloured '*kamar-band*' (sash). Occasionally Pangwālās may like to put on vest-coat over the woollen shirt instead of a coat. In local vernacular the *koṭh* is also known as *likkaḍ* or *likkar*. *Likkaḍ* in Chamba dialect means fragments of clothes, while in old Chamba dialect and in Churāh *likkaḍ* or *likkar* signifies sewn garments.

2.5. Mājhin (Kamar-band, Paṭkā)

It is a black or dark pink coloured broad striped woollen cloth, wrapped around the waist and is two metres in length. It is a simplified version of *ḍorās* of Gaddis. The Hindi dictionary defines *mājjhanā* as tucking in between. The *mājjhanā* thus rightly is an apparel for the middle part of the body. *Mājhin* is undoubtedly a derivative or a distorted form of *mājjhanā*.

2.6. Pulāns or Pullay

Pulāns (straw-shoes) are locally prepared from straw and hemp-yarn. The shoes do not last for more than a few months, but their utility is great. In winter they do not slip over the hard snow, and secondly they are cosy and keep the feet warm. *Pulāns* are used by both males and females of Pāngi valley. In Chamba district, it is also pronounced as *pulā*. *Pulā* is a Sanskrit word and occurs in the Vedas where it signifies long boots.

3. Costumes of Pangwālans (women)

A Pangwālan is renowned for her beauty amongst all the women-folk of Chamba. The cold climate of the upper regions helps in preserving her fair complexion. Her dress is feminine and graceful.

3.1. Joji

The *joji* deserves a place of pride for making Pangwālan an irresistible enchantress. The ancient scriptures compare the cunningness and the gait, the anger and the fury of a woman with that of serpent. The *joji* is a kind of head-dress, which reminds one of a hooded cobra. It is a sort of flat cloth cap with a long tail of cloth hanging down from its back. The tail is broad at the top and gradually narrows down to a point at the tail end. The Pangwālan wears *joji* on her head with the tail part hanging at the back. It is made of colourful, embroidered cotton cloth. An older cap of thick *paṭṭu* is also worn by some of the middle-aged women.

3.2. Choli

Choli of Pangwālan is a full-sleeved shirt with a collar and is made of either printed or plain handloom cloth available in the market. It is also made of woollen *paṭṭu* cloth. It is also called a '*choie*'.

3.3. Chālaṇ (Chuḍidār Suthan)

The trousers known as *chālaṇ* of a Pangwālan are loose at the thighs but gradually turn tighter till they reach down the ankels. These trousers are full of puckers down below.

3.4. Chādru and Khesh

The *chādru* is a woollen sheet while the *khesh* is a cotton sheet bought from the market. The *chādru* is prepared from wool procured locally. In both the cases the length of the cloth is 4 to 4.50 metres. It is an unstitched garb. The *chādru* and *khesh* are worn around the body in a peculiar but very graceful manner. One end of it is brought over the left shoulder and the blanket is then passed behind the back under the right arm, and across the breast, where it is fixed at the left shoulder by a large brass or silver pin. It is then passed under the left arm and across the back, to the front of the right shoulder where it is again fastened with another brass or silver pin. The ends hang down in the front from each shoulder giving the wearer a very attractive look.

Mention here may also be made of a minor tribe of Pāngi, the Bhoṭs. The Bhoṭs are Buddhist, but their life-style is not much different from the Pangwālās. In dress the only point of distinction found is a long and loose coat which may even cover the ankles. It faintly resembles the under-gown '*sanghaṭi*', worn by Buddhist monks. On special occasions Bhoṭlies (Bhoṭ women) may dress themselves like Pangwālans.

5

COSTUMES OF CHURĀHĪS

1. CHURĀHĪS

The ancient name of Churāh tehsil seems to be 'Chaturāh', meaning crossroads. The people of Churāh came from primitive nomadic tribes. A good part of the community, some scholars believe, seems to have migrated from Central Asia more than a thousand years ago. The history of Churāh points out to that area being culturally isolated much of the time. But its isolation was never total at least after 13th century A.D., judged by the character of change in their religious belief. At present Churāhīs represent a mixture of diverse cultures added and adopted from time to time. The generic name of the residents of Churāh tehsil is Churāhīs, which also include Gaddis and Busheharis.[1] Gujjars are also the residents of Churāh. The major castes of Churāhīs consist of Brahmins, Rajputs, Halis, Aryas, Musalmans, Lohārs and Rathis, etc. In fact, a large part of the population of Mohammedans in Chamba district is concentrated in Churāh tehsil.

The typical nomadic residential house throughout Churāh is small and square structure and is built of a flat roof known as *saraṇ*.[2] It is plastered inside and outside with a durable type of mud. The base of the flat-roofed *saraṇ* is made of timber planks which are covered with a four to six inches thick mixture of mud,

---

1. People who migrated from the princely state of Rampur Bushehar of Upper Shimla hills.
2. *Saraṇ* is a Hindi word which means refuge.

sticks and leaves. Most of the flat-roofed houses contain only one or two rooms and a small door-way. There is a small window near the ceiling for ventilation and there is a provision for chimney known as *dhuānkhu* also in the roof. The room itself is closed on all sides. The flat roof is used for basking in the sun and other household chores.

The economy of Churāh is based primarily on agriculture. Other secondary traditional economic pursuits are hunting and weaving (blankets and *paṭṭu* cloth with designs), basketry and bee-keeping. Horticulture in the near future is likely to become a major source of income due to ample plantation of apple orchards these days. To sum up, the economy of Churāh that emerges is typical of a peasant society in an under-developed but modernising country of the temperate zone.

The fountain stone slabs of Churāh (11th-13th century A.D.) are carved with the figures of god Varuna, river goddesses Ganga and Yamuna and other early Indian decorative motifs of Vedic age. This could mean that the builders of these fountain slabs, i.e. Ranas and Thakurs, entered Churāh well before the Christian era. Once here they were more or less isolated from the new religious priests who were well versed in post-Vedic beliefs and rituals, until after 13th century A.D., as one continues to find early Vedic period motifs on these fountain stone slabs down to 12th-13th century A.D.

The people of Churāh speak Churāhī, Churāhī-gādī and Bushehari dialects.

2. Costumes of Churāhīs (men)

The costumes of Churāhīs do not differ much from that of Gaddis of Brahmour, except for the head-dress.

2.1. Sāfā, Ṭop

The head-dress of Churāhīs is ordinary and simple looking turban which is worn in most parts of India as well. It is a long sheet of cloth, tied around the head in numerous folds, and is locally called *sāfā.* Occasionally the Churāhīs may also go in for a skull-cap known as '*ṭop*', which is lighter and easy to wear. In winter season they wear '*ḳan-ṭop*' with long flaps to cover ears.

2.2. Kameej

It is an ordinary shirt made of light material. In winter a Churāhī may clothe himself with a loose woollen shirt upto the knee length.

2.3. Suthan (Pyjāmā)

Churāhī trousers known as *suthan* may be either made of cotton or wool. The garment is loose above but tight at the legs and ankles but not puckered up into folds as is the case in Brahmour.

2.4. Cholā, Ḍorā and Coat

Over the shirt a *cholā* is worn, which is like that of a Gaddi *cholā*, and is tied around the waist with *ḍorā*. The Churāhīs use this dress on special occasions such as *Jātra*, fair and festivals. For ordinary use a Churāhī wears a long coat coming upto his knees. This coat is made of woollen *paṭṭu* and is usually tied around the waist with long flap of cloth known as '*paṭkā*' (sash).

2.5. Bāsket

Over the shirt but underneath the coat Churāhīs clothe themselves with a *bāsket*, which for all intents and purposes is similar to modern vest-coat.

2.6. Juṭṭā (Shoes)

In local dialect the name for Churāhīs *juṭṭā* is *paṇi*, which is distorted version of Hindi word *Panhī* implying shoes. The Churāhīs wear open shoes of untanned raw leather, which are hard and sturdy, and well suited for the rough hilly journey. These shoes are locally prepared.

3. Costumes of Churāhans (women)

The costumes of Churāhans are much more interesting than that of their male counterpart. Many of the ancient fountain stone slabs in this region hint at the antiquity of their dress and reveal their striking features.

3.1. Head-dress

(a) Joji

It is a flat cap of cloth with a narrow rounded rim. This *joji* is slightly larger than that of Pangwālan, but in all other respects it resembles the Pangwālan *joji*. According to Hermann Goetz:

> ". . . . this flat cap is found amongst the Hunza women of Hindu Kush, the Kurdish women of Persia and the Circarsion women of Carcasus."[1]

He traces its origin from Mongol period and medieval Europe (13th century A.D.). Its origin according to him can be further traced to an east Iranian prototype as it is a common head-dress of the Bactrians, and even of the Persian kings of Achaemenia.

(b) Dupaṭṭā or Chādru

It is a piece of unstitched coloured cloth which is thrown over the head and then wrapped around the shoulders. *Chādru* may also be wrapped like a turban when a woman is carrying things over her head or when she is working in the fields, so that it does not obstruct her activities. *Dupaṭṭā* when wrapped like this protects

1. Hermann Goetz, *The Early Wooden Temples of Chamba*, Leiden (1955), p. 47.

her hair also. Now-a-days silken or synthetic *chādru* is preferred to a cotton one.

3.2. Kameej (Choli)

Kameej of a Churāhan is like a short bodice reaching upto her waist. It is prepared from an ordinary cloth, with full sleeves and with cuffs and collars. It is also called '*choli*'.

3.3. Bāsket

Over the *kameej* a vest-coat is worn by Churāhī women, which consists of two similar pieces kept together by angular broaches. This garment (*bāsket*) resembles the commonly used Indian *choli* (brassiere), or a sleeveless sewn jacket, or a vest-coat which are also worn instead by Churāhī women. The same costume is found in use among the Gujjars also as far as they have not yet adopted Punjabi or Kashmiri dress.

3.4. Ḍoḍ

The Hindi dictionary defines *dohar* as a sheet or a blanket, the parts of which are sewn together. *Ḍoḍ* is the desorted form of *dohar*. *Ḍoḍ* is made of two sheets of blankets sewn into one to make the breadth sufficient to cover the lower parts of the body. It is wrapped around the waist covering the entire lower limbs. At the sides the *ḍoḍ* is again folded slightly so that both the sides overlap the front portion of the thighs. The *ḍoḍ* is prepared locally especially for this purpose and is of black colour with a check or striped pattern. It is also known by the name of *likker* or *kambli*. Its length is about 2.50 metres. The *ḍoḍ* can serve as a bedsheet for use in the open pasture lands also.

3.5. Paṭkā

The *ḍoḍ* is held together with the help of a waist-band known as *kamar-band*, tied at the waist. It is a white sheet of cloth, 2½ metres in length. The *kamar-band* here is called *paṭkā* or *gātri*.

3.6. Chuḍyāli

Chuḍyāli is a pair of trousers also called '*suthan chuḍidār*' and likens a tight *pyjāmā* with puckers. The etymology of word *chuḍyāli* is probably from the Chameālī word *chuḍi* signifying like folds.

3.7. Paṇi

Paṇi is *desi juṭṭā*, a kind of shoes without any laces. Sometimes it may be embroidered with silk and *goṭṭa*. Even till today the *pulāns* which are prepared out of straws and hemp yarn are being used by both male and female.

Mention may here also be made of a minor tribe of Busheharies, which number a few hundred and had migrated from Rampur-Bushehar state in Shimla hills a long time ago. Their dress is similar to Churāhīs except for distinct type of a cap or a *ṭopi* called '*Bushehari-ṭopi*', which identifies them as a separate clan.

6

COSTUMES OF CHAMBYĀLS

1. CHAMBYĀLS

The generic term for the inhabitants of Chamba tehsil is Chambyāls or Chamyāls. Chamba came into existence in 10th century A.D. Raja Sahila Varman, the founder of the town Chamba, was accompanied by his Gaddi subjects and Gaddi army. Hence it can be presumed that Chamba in 10th century A.D. was inhabited primarily by the Gaddis. Raja Sahila Verman had to subjugate the petty chieftains of the lower Ravi valley who were known by the name of Ranas and Thakurs. Possibly, in early 10th century A.D. the place might have been inhabited by Ranas, Thakurs and Rathis and their low-caste subjects. The idol (bronze) of Hari Rai (Vaikunṭh-murti) in Hari Rai temple which is still under worship belongs to 8th-9th century A.D. A study of the architecture of the fragments of a brick temple (built 6th century A.D.[1]) discovered in Chamba proper (now preserved in Bhuri Singh Museum, Chamba), during an excavation, also indicates that in Chamba a certain settlement flourished before 10th century A.D., of which no other vestiges are known.

Probably Chamba also formed a part of Audumbara republic in 2nd century B.C. The discovery of Indo-Greek coins (Ist century B.C.) at Lachoḍi village situated in the close vicinity of Chamba[2]

1. Hermann Goetz, *Studies in the History and Art of Kashmir and the Indian Himalaya*, Wiesbaden (1969), p. 131.
2. V.C. Ohri, *Art of Himachal*, State Museum, Simla (1975), p. 218.

alludes to the existence of this place even during those turbulent times.

The Brahmins of Chamba claim themselves to be the inhabitants of the town from very ancient period. Their claim rests on the founder of Chamba having taken the land from the Kanwāṇ-Brahmins who were the original settlers there. Some notable Brahmin families also came from Kashmir and Kulu. Some learned Bengali Brahmin families well versed in tantra are reputed to have been brought to Chamba from Benaras by Raja Ganesh Varman in 1558 A.D. The notable personages of this family were Pandit Suranand and Ramapati, who were appointed 'Rajguru' and minister respectively. As regards the other Brahmin families it is probable that many of them began to find their way into the hills at an early period as priests and religious devotees.[1]

A good majority of Rajputs in Chamba are 'mians'. Twenty princes of Rajputs clan were kept as hostages in the Mughal court during Jahangir's period. They were referred to as 'mians'. The term Chambyāl also includes Khatris, Jāts, Mahajans, Sikhs and Mohammedans etc. They must all have come from the plains of Punjab and Kangra, probably at not very remote period. Chamba also had its own influx of population brought by the partition of India in 1947 A.D. in the form of large number of displaced persons from Pārāchanār now in Pakistan.

The people of Chamba tehsil speak Chameālī, Dogri, Gādī-Chameālī, Gādī-Hindi, Gujjari and Pārāchanāri.

2. Costumes of Chambyāls (Men)

2.1. Jāmā, Garkhi, Chuḍidār Suthan, Paṭkā and Sāfā

During the period of Mughal rulers Shahjahan and Aurangzeb (1627-1707 A.D.), men of upper classes all over northern India

1. J. Hutchison and J.P.H. Vogel, *History of the Punjab Hill States*, Vol. I, Lahore (1933), p. 273.

wore the type of dresses which were in vogue in the Mughal court, with slight variation suitable to the local needs and conditions.

In Chamba, the upper classes, the courtiers and the princes wore a kind of *jāmā*. This *jāmā* can still be seen in some of the old houses of Chamba. The *jāmā* was a dress reserved for special occasions. It is amusing to note that the *jāmā* worn by the Chamba people is a refined version of the Gaddi *cholā*. *Jāmā* was a full sleeved garment, worn crosswise above the waist to the right. One frontal flap overlapped the other and was held together by means of buttons made of cloth. The length of *jāmā* reached below the knees. It was prepared from the finest woollen material and was embroidered.

Along with *jāmā* another popular dress with the subjects of Chamba was *angarkhā*. In local dialects it was called '*garkhi*'. The *angarkhā* was sewn tight at the torso but below the waist it had an open fall exactly like a modern skirt. Along with *angarkhā* a pair of trousers known as *chuḍidār suthan* '*reb-dar*' of *gulbadan* (a kind of striped silk cloth) was worn. The *chuḍidār suthan* was similar to the famous Jodhpur trousers tight up to the ankles and baggy above the knees. The *angarkhā* was tied at the waist with *paṭkā* (sash) 2.50 metres in length. This *paṭkā* is also called '*lak*'.

A *chādar* (sheet) was wrapped around the shoulders. To complete the full garb a turban (*pagḍi*) was tied around the head. The *pagḍi* unlike the modern *pagḍi* consisted of comparatively shorter piece of cloth and was tied around the head by giving symmetrical turns, so that one fold was placed exactly over the other, leaving only a little margin. Later on the *pagḍi* was dropped in favour of *sāfā* or a full-length turban.

Sāfā was also worn along with shirt, *pyjāmā* and coat etc. Even now the elderly men of Chamba are seen wearing *sāfā*. During the royal times to walk with uncovered head was viewed with displeasure.

We have no evidence of the kind of dress worn by the Chambyāls during the Muslim period. But it is commonly believed that before the regime of Raja Ganesh Varman (1512-1559 A.D.) the dress of the Chambyāls was the one worn by Gaddis. In 1558 A.D. Pandit Suranand and Pandit Ramapati, who were brought by Raja Ganesh Varman, did many reforms in every sphere of the state. Before this there was 'Gaddi-chalā', meaning thereby Gaddi system or 'as the Gaddis do'. After that period, the Muslim influence became discernible, and that became quite evident in dress habits too as stated above.

2.2. Chogā, Chuḍidār Pyjāmā and Sāfā (Court-dress)

The court-dress of Chamba worn by the nobles, princes and high officials of the state consisted of a turban, a *chogā* and *chuḍidār pyjāmā.* This dress was worn by state officials to attend 'durbar', royal procession or any other state function. *Sāfā* made from silk and finest cotton muslin or *malmal*, was used at these occasions. The most favoured and cherished *sāfā* was silken 'banārsi' one. The *chogā* was a full length garment made from the *jari* cloth and silk. The *chogā* of *jari* cloth was applied with *goṭṭā* work. The silken *chogā* was worn by the Raja and other high nobles and officials. It was superior to *jari chogā* and was embroidered with gold and silver threads. Often the *chogā* of Raja and his princes was studded with costly diamonds and pearls. The turban of the Raja was also decorated with festoon strings of golds. According to Dr. V.C. Ohri, the tradition of wearing *chogā* in Chamba can be traced to the *chogā* worn in Lucknow of Avadh Nawābs. Along with *chogā* a shirt and *chuḍidār pyjāmā* was worn. Underneath the *chogā*, was worn an embroidered vest-coat. The above dress was also worn by the *Bārātis* during the marriage processions of Chambyāls.

So far we have discussed the style of dresses of the upper class Chambyāls. The local gentry, which consists of merchants, shop-keepers, local professionals and commoners were content with a simple shirt, *pyjāmā*, coat and *sāfā* or *ṭopi* over the head.

2.3. Footwear

The *paṇi* (shoes) for royalty were prepared from the untarnished fine new leather, and were embroidered with silk thread and *tillā* work. Chamba *chappal* (sandals) has also come in vogue during the British regime. *Chappal* and *mozā* (socks) both made from leather were also used in the snowy season.

3. Costumes of Chambyālans (women)

During the invasion of Muslims into the north Indian plains there was not much infiltration of foreign dress in Chamba area, and the numerous fountain slabs found in the region (11th to 13th century A.D.) reveal *choli* and *ghāgrā* as the main female dress. This dress is still in use in some tehsils and parganas of Chamba, i.e. in Sahoo, Panjla, Karad etc. The *choli* here has taken the shape of a small shirt with full sleeves reaching upto waist, and from waist down a *ghāgrā* is worn which is prepared from woollen *paṭṭu* cloth. It was during the Mughal period when the dress of Chambyāls underwent a complete change. A fountain stone slab procured from a distant village of Chamba, shows the figurines wearing Mughal dress. This slab is dated 1608-1707 A.D. The figurines on this slab wear *jāmā*. Perhaps the engraver of this slab had escaped to the hills due to the persecution policy of Aurangzeb. Alternatively the local engraver might have seen the acceptance and frequent use of Mughal dress among ruling classes of Chamba, who evidently had been the patrons of such works of art and dedication.

3.1. Peshwāj

The *peshwāj* was used in the Mughal court often as a ceremonial dress. It is a gown-like frock reaching from the neck down to the ankels with long sleeves and often with a narrow waist. The waist line of the costume commences from below the bosom. This dress arrived in Chamba probably prior to 1780 A.D. It is one of the heaviest garments, requiring about 27 to 36 metres of cloth. The *peshwāj* of Chamba is sleeveless. The fall from the waist is full and circumference at the ankles very big (45 to 54 metres).

The *peshwāj* is prepared out of *laṭhā* variety of cotton cloth. After the *peshwāj* is sewn it is sent to the dyer for colouring. Red has been the colour of choice of Chamba womenfolk. The *peshwāj* was a dress full of grandeaur, reminding one of the glory of by-gone days. After dying the *peshwāj* in red colour, *goṭṭā* and other applique work was applied to it. This sort of *peshwāj* was especially used for marriage ceremonies, and during fairs and festivals. The *peshwāj* became extremely popular amongst the ladies of Chamba and it is still worn today. We believe that nowhere else in India a female Mughal dress is still worn in its original form. In the wardrobe of Chamba ladies usually two types of *peshwāj* were preserved. One was a simple or *sādā* variety which was used for ordinary occasions like paying a visit to the next door neighbour. The other kind of *peshwāj* decorated with *goṭṭā* work was reserved for special occasions. For winter the *peshwāj* was prepared from finest woollen *paṭṭu* and was called *cholu*, which resembled the *cholu* of Gaddi women.

Etymology of the word *peshwāj* can be traced to an ancient word *pesās* occurring in Vedic literature, connoting embroidered garments. However, according to Charles Fabri the word *peshwāj* is derived from *Pasujnā*, meaning stitching. It may be mentioned here that *peshwāj* ever remained a formal dress for Chamba ladies to be worn on occasions and essentially while going outdoors. Within their own household Chamba ladies never wore a *peshwāj*, and taking off the *peshwāj* was the first thing to be done on entering one's house.

3.2. Dupaṭṭā

Along with *peshwāj*, a *dupaṭṭā* was worn over the head which was either of '*gokharu*', '*goṭhṇi*' or '*dhankāwālā*' type. The main feature

.1. Female figures from fountain stone slab of Churāh, 11th cent. A.D. revealing stitched garments resembling *Choli* and *Ghāgrā* (Courtesy Bhuri Singh Museum, Chamba).

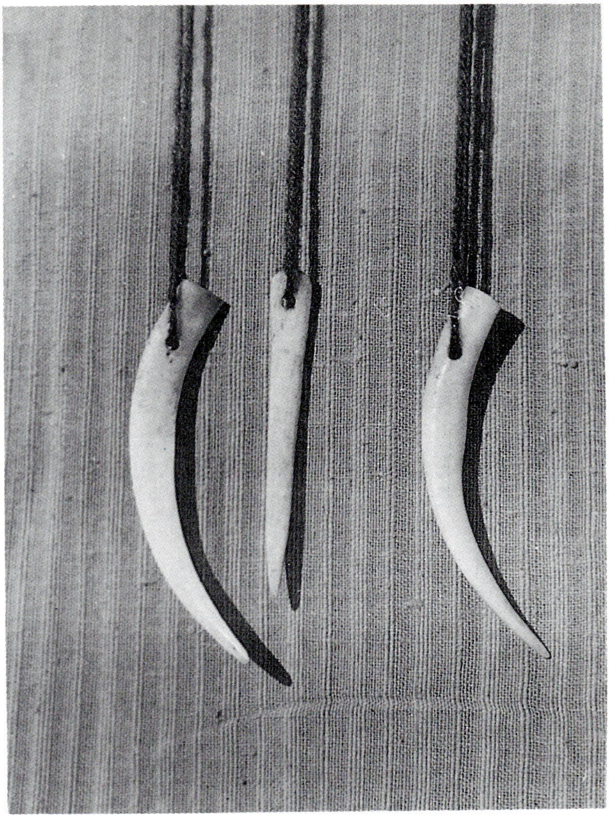

A2. Needles of sheep or goat-bones and musk-deer fangs.

A3. Lady spinning wool on *charkhā*.

A4. Weaving *paṭṭu* (woollen cloth) on family handloom known as *rachh*.

A5. Bronze image of master sculptor Guggā (7th century A.D.) (Courtesy Bhuri Singh Museum, Chamba).

A6. Figure of a donor in Indo-Scythian dress, resembling with Gaddi *cholā* (over-coat), *ṭop* (peaked cap), *suthan* (trousers) (Kushān sculpture, Mathura Museum).

A7. Figures from fountain stone slab, 11th century A.D., donning dress faintly resembling Scythian garments (Courtesy Bhuri Singh Museum, Chamba).

A8. Carved figure of Raja Prithvi Singh of Chamba (1641-1664 A.D.) on wooden door showing him in Mughal costume and holding royal insignia of fish known as a māhī-o-marātib (Courtesy Bhuri Singh Museum, Chamba).

A9. Painting of Wazir Bagha in Sikh costume shown with Gaddi petitioner (mid-19th century A.D.) (Courtesy Bhuri Singh Museum, Chamba).

A10. A Gaddi functionary of the State.

A11. A Gaddi wearing a *ṭop* (peaked cap).

A12. A Gaddi couple in their traditional dress.

A13. *Baglu* (leather bag) with *ruṇkā* (flint-lock).

A14. *Jaḍulā* (goat-hair boots).

15. Gaddi women husking paddy with wooden clubs known as *mohal*.

A16. Gaddi belle in her traditional finery.

A17. Decorative mirror to be fastened on the *ḍora*.

A18. Gujjar kid wearing a peculiar cap having a peaked top, called Gujjari *ṭopi.*

A19. Gujjar in his traditional dress.

A20. Gujjar woman in her traditional dress.

A21. Gujjar lady wearing a head-dress called *joji*.

A22. Pangwlālā in his traditional dress.

A23. Traditional dress of a Pangi woman.

A24. Cap worn by Pangi women known as *joji*.

A25. Straw shoes called *pulān*.

A26. Embroidered laced leather foot-wear and leather socks known as *mozā* and *chappal* (Courtesy Bhuri Singh Museum, Chamba).

A27. Group photograph of Churāhī women in their tribal costumes.

A28. Ceremonial dress worn in Chamba proper (*sāfā, chogā, pyjāmā*).

A29. Embroidered leather foot-wear known as *paṇi*
(Courtesy Bhuri Singh Museum, Chamba).

A30. Two ladies, one wearing printed skirt known as *ghāgrā* and other wearing long over-coat known as *peshwāj*.

A31. Chamba costume *peshwāj* and *dupaṭṭā*.

A32. Embroidered bodice known as *choli*.

A33. Group photograph showing the residents of Bhaṭṭiyāt with musical instruments.

A34. A woman in black *ghāgrā*.

A35. A woman of Bhaṭṭiyāt with her children.

A36. Gaddi lady donning silver and gold ornaments.

of *gokharuwālā dupaṭṭā* was that it was decorated with *goṭṭā* work done all over in criss-cross fashion. The *goṭhṇiwālā dupaṭṭā* was bordered with piping of different colours. The *dhankāwālā dupaṭṭā* was bordered with three or four strips of *goṭṭā* running all around the border.

3.3. Choli, Ghāgrā, Oḍhani

The young women of Chamba wore the seductive dress *choli, ghāgrā* and *oḍhani*. The *choli* was often a backless, half-sleeved, embroidered garment tied at the back with laces. To cover the lower limbs a *ghāgrā* (skirt) often striped or embossed was worn, tied at the waist with a string. This *ghāgrā* had close resemblance with the modern petticoat. Over the head an *oḍhani* (*orhani*) was thrown casually, its fall was tucked into the waist band and gathered in front of the *ghāgrā*. It is this enchanting dress which is revealed in hundreds of Kangra and Chamba paintings. Women wearing this type of dress can still be seen in Saho, Panjla and Karad parganas of Chamba tehsil, but here *choli* has now become a short shirt with full sleeves.

The *choli, ghāgrā* and *oḍhani* were perhaps later on destined to be the precursor of the modern '*sāri*'. In some of the Kangra paintings this transitional period from *ghāgrā*, *choli* to '*sāri*' is discernible. Recorded examples of the *choli*, the bodice or blouse are found in the pre-Mughal miniature paintings of Gujarat, but there was gradual adoption of *choli* in northern India. It is the first example of an upper garment for a woman. It covered only the front, the back being bare, a type of blouse that can be found in many parts of northern India.

3.4. Suthan, Kameej and Dupaṭṭā

Another kind of dress worn by the Chamba women was *dupaṭṭā, kameej* and *suthan*. The *kameej* (shirt) is of *kaliwāli* (*kaliḍār*) which is narrow up to the waist, but has elongated sides like 'Lucknavi *kurtā*'. It is seldom decorated with *goṭṭā* work. The *kameej* could be a simple one also. The *kameej kaliwāli* is without collars but the *sādā kurtā* is with collars and cuffs. Along with this kind of *kurtā*, a *suthan chuḍidār* is worn. It is made of *gulbadan* kind of cloth and is either of deep red colour or of parrot green colour.

Now-a-days modern *sāri* dress or *shalwār* (*salwār*) or *pyjāmā* and shirts of different fashions are worn by Chamba womenfolk. Shawls are also wrapped around the shoulders.

3.5. Footwear

The *paṇi* (*juṭṭi*) worn by Chamba women was analogous to modern slippers but embroidered in the forefront with silk and *goṭṭā*. In the current times the *paṇi* is discarded in favour of the modern class of footwear. The typical ladies Chamba *chappal* still finds favour and is the main attraction for the Chamba women.

7

Costumes of Bhaṭṭiyāls

1. Bhaṭṭiyāls

The Bhaṭṭiyāt tehsil is probably named after the Bhaṭṭi caste which predominates this area.[1] The ancient name of Bhaṭṭiyāt tehsil was Bhaṭṭi. The inhabitants of this area were warriors of repute, and the Bhaṭṭi as such always remained the recruiting ground for the Chamba army. The Wazarat or state sub-division of Bhaṭṭi is often indicated by the name of 'Bārā-Bhaṭṭian', which points to its having once consisted of twelve parganas,[2] meaning thereby twelve different establishments (abodes) of twelve different Bhaṭṭis or tribes. According to Cunningham, "the Bhaṭṭis are Yadavas of acknowledged descent through the far-famed 'Krishna'. The original name for a tribe was Bhaṭṭi and this name is still held by the Hindu Yadavas of Jaisalmer".[3] In pre-British Punjab also Bhaṭṭis and Missels denoted different warrior tribes of the area.

The greater part of the tract between the Hathi-Dhār and Dhaula-Dhār lies in the Beas valley, and with the addition of a small portion of the lower Ravi valley Bhaṭṭiyāt tehsil of Chamba is formed, which in proportion to its size is the most popular and fertile sub-division of the district.

---

1. J.P.H. Vogel, *Antiquities of Chamba State,* Part I, Calcutta (1911), p. 5.
2. Ibid., p. 13.
3. Alexander Cunningham, *Archaeological Survey of India,* Simla (1871), p. 19.

Raja Sahila Varman (10th century A.D.) had conquered Trigarta (Kangra) and annexed the whole southern fringe of the ranges from Ravi to Bir Bhangāl.[1] There are said to be many traditions in Kangra pointing to an early occupation of these territories by the Chamba king. While advancing towards Bir Bhangāl the Raja brought under his control the territory of Bhaṭṭiyāt which was then occupied by Ranas and Thakurs.

The territory of Bhaṭṭiyāt has always remained an apple of discord between the Raja of Chamba and the Kangra and Nurpur rulers, and, as a result, Bhaṭṭiyāt changed hands many a time during the course of its known history.

The territories of Bhaṭṭiyāt also included the areas which now form part of Dalhousie town and Bakloh cantonment. Dalhousie was set up by the British in 1851 A.D., with a view to establishing a sanitarium and convalescent depot for British soldiers and for the Europeans. The Bakloh plateau was transferred to the British in 1866 A.D. for setting up a Gurkha cantonment. Consequently, there was a considerable fusion of races and culture in that region. The majority of the population of Bakloh and Kakirā consists of Gurkhas (Nepalis) who settled there with their families as ex-servicemen.

Bhaṭṭiyāl now is a generic term used for the inhabitants of Bhaṭṭi or Bhaṭṭiyāt tehsil and include all classes of people, such as Gaddis, Gurkhas and Mahajans besides the original Brahmins, Rajputs and other agricultural and working classes. Gujjars also inhabit this area. These castes include, Brahmins, Rajputs, Mahajans, Ad-Dharmis or Ravidasis, Dhogris (who burn and prepare charcoal), Khatries, Mahāshyas, Ḍoomnas, Hālis, Musalmans and Kolis. The Bhaṭṭiyāls maintain their family links with the Kangra people and Dogras of Jammu, and, as such, have a cultural affinity with that of the people of Kangra and Jammu. Geographically also

1. Thakur Sen Negi, *District Gazetteer Chamba* (1963), p. 112.

these areas are contiguous, and access to Jammu and Kangra from Bhaṭṭiyāt is both easier and nearer than any other part of Chamba district. Bhaṭṭiyāls speak Bhaṭeāli, Bhaṭeāli-Gādī, Gurkhali (Nepali), Punjabi, Dogri and of course Kangri.

2. Costumes of Bhaṭṭiyāls (men)

The climate of Bhaṭṭiyāt tehsil is comparatively hotter and full of humidity as compared to other parts of Chamba during rains. The territory of Bhaṭṭiyāt lies adjacent to Kangra district and Jammu, and there is considerable fusion and intermingling in their life styles including that of their dresses. Gujjar, Gaddi and Gurkha families inhabiting Bhaṭṭiyāt, however, wear their own type of distinct dresses.

The Bhaṭṭiyāls in general wear *pyjāmā, kurtā*, vest-coat, coat and turban. While working in the fields they take off their entire clothes except for their under-wears so that they can work unhindered, these do not get soiled and primarily because of comparatively warmer and more hospitable climate conditions. Bhaṭṭiyāls are the only people in whole of Chamba who wear only under-garments while working in the fields. It was perhaps for this reason that people from other parts of Chamba derisively called Bhaṭṭiyāls as '*nangjanghu*' or bare-legged. Over their '*kachhas*' (under-wear) Bhaṭṭiyāls would sometimes wrap a piece of cloth akin to a half-*dhoti* which is called *paḍtaṇi* (*partni*—that which is folded) in local dialect. While moving out they may wrap a *paḍtaṇi* around their neck or make it hang loose over the shoulders. The *paḍtaṇi* is in fact a multipurpose garment used as a *dhoti*, a towel, a handkerchief, a cover and even a carrier for the goods purchased in the market. The Bhaṭṭiyāls will use it as handkerchief while travelling or as receptacle for depositing some eatables or few coins. They also wrap around their shoulders a white sheet of cloth known as *chādar*, which serves the function and utility of a shawl. They wear shoes (*juṭṭā*), and *desi chappals* as footwear while moving out.

Components of Dress (already discussed earlier)

1. *Sāfā* and *ṭopi* (turban and cap)
2. *Kameej (kurtā), sādā* or *kaliwāli* (shirts)
3. Coat, *bāsket* (coat, vest-coat)
4. *Pyjāmās, suthan, dhoti* or *paḍtaṇi* (for lower limbs)
5. *Juṭṭā* and *chappals* (shoes)
6. *Paḍtaṇi*—a small sheet of cloth, 1.50 metres long and 50 cms wide, used as a scarf around the neck or hung over the shoulders.
7. *Chadār*—a sheet of cloth 2 to 2.50 metres long and 46 cms wide, used as shawl.

3. Costumes of Bhaṭṭiyālans (women)

The Bhaṭṭiyālans are seen wearing a wide skirt—*ghāgri* or *shalwār* which is the same as prevalent in Punjab. The border of *ghāgri* is decorated with a strap bearing colourful designs, or the whole garment is made of streaks of colours tastefully arranged. *Choli* covers the upper part of the body and is used with *ghāgri*. Here *choli* in fact is short shirt reaching up to waist having full sleeves.

Another dress for the lower part of the body is *suthan chuḍidār* (tight trousers), but now it has fallen into disuse and only the old women might use it at times. With *shalwār*, a *kameej* is worn, which is a long full-sleeved shirt extended upto the knees. For head-gear a *dupaṭṭā, chādru* or *hariḍā* is used, which is either *gokharuwālā* or *sādā. Dupaṭṭā* is worn with every type of dress, because tradition demands that every woman should cover her head. Married ladies do not use white *dupaṭṭā,* which is reserved for widows only. On festive occasions a Bhaṭṭiyālan puts on new clothes. The footwear mainly consist of *chappals* and sandals.

Components of Dress (mentioned earlier)

1. *Dupaṭṭā, Chādru, Hariḍā (Gokhruwālā dupaṭṭā)* (head-dress)
2. *Kurtā-Kaliwālā* or *Kameej* (shirt)

3. *Suthan Chuḍiwāli, Shalwār phairdār* (lower limb garments)
4. *Ghāgri, Choli* (skirt and blouse)
5. *Juṭṭi, Chappals* etc. (footwear).

4. Costumes of Gurkhas (Nepalis)

4.1. Men

The Gurkhas as such do not constitute the original tribe of Chamba. A Gurkha cantonment was established by the British in 1866 A.D. at Bakloh, and the present population are the descendants of Gurkha families set up by the Britishers during the course of the century. Their way of life is entirely different from the rest of the population and they have no affinities with other tribes of Chamba. A Gurkha adorns his head with a black cap popularly known as Gurkhali or Nepali *ṭopi*. It resembles a hull of a ship.

He wears a long white shirt and a *chuḍidār pyjāmā*. Over this white garb, a black vest-coat is worn. To make the dress complete, any black or dark coloured coat is put on. Sometimes in place of a vest-coat, a sort of white gown, *daurā*, is also worn over this dress. The gown is tied with a waist-band, *paṭṭukā* or *kamar-paṭṭā.*

Components of Dress:

1. Nepali or Gurkhāli *ṭopi* (cap)
2. *Kameej* (white long shirt)
3. *Daurā* ('*cholā*' type gown)
4. *Pyjāmā Chuḍidār* (trouser)
5. *Bāsket* (vest-coat black)
6. Coat
7. *Paṭṭukā, Kamar-paṭṭā* (white waist band).

4.2. Women

Coming from a different land, a Gurkha woman is no mean beauty.

For head-gear a *rumāl* is tied around the head by giving a knot at the back like a '*dhaṭhu*'. The main dress and in fact the only dress of a Gurkha woman is blouse, *sāri* and *rumāl*. Blouse is a sort of a small shirt full-sleeved and reaching down upto the waist. A *sāri* is wrapped to cover the lower limbs. The *sāri* is worn in a very simple manner and no petticoat is essentially worn underneath. Unlike Hindustani *sāri* there are no folds and falls, and no end of *sāri* is passed over the shoulders to conceal the breasts.

Components of Dress

1. *Rumāl* (head-gear)
2. Blouse
3. *Sāri*.

PART II

ORNAMENTS

8

ORNAMENTS

Love of jewellery and ornaments is inherent in mankind. To a Hindu, beauty is not only an absolute but a relative concept as well and it must be evident to the senses and intelligence. The beginning of jewellery in this country is lost in hoary past, and in our quest for ancient and primitive jewellery, we must turn to the tribes of the hills. Even before the advent of Aryans into the hills, the aboriginals of this area used different techniques and material for self-ornamentation. The Aryans were equally fond of ornaments. The main ornaments which their deities wore were *Akshya-mālā, Vanamālā, Vaijanti-mālā, rudraksha-mālā, muṇḍ-mālā* of Śiva etc. The Vedas, the Ramayana and many ancient texts carry elaborate description as to the gold and silver ornaments. Besides Mohen-jo-daro and Harappa and other excavations have also brought to light many highly artistic and finished ornaments.

The foothills of the Himalaya abound in numerous rivulets, streams and fountains. These watersheds served as meeting places for the tribal folks, which gathered there for watering their animals, for taking bath and for other daily needs. They were fascinated by the stones of different colours and hues shining under the surface of water. They felt immense pleasure in making a necklace of them and putting them around their neck. Possibly this practice was the beginning of human interest in gems and other kinds of stones. The aboriginals also decorated their bodies by means of different kinds of wood, fresh flowers, petals, fruits and other specimen from the world of vegetation. Even till the present times, the ornaments of the human race bear the impression, designs and motifs derived from the world of nature, such as, flowers, petals, creepers, sea-shells, fruits, birds, animals, etc.

Even now, in the far-flung areas of Chamba the tribal folk adorn their bodies with the *hār* (necklace) made out of nuts of hilly apricot fruit locally called *chir*. The necklace is specially prepared for *jātras* and is sold by the local people. A custom which is now falling in disuse, but was once popular in the female society about a decade ago, was the adorning of ears by a pair of artificial black or white curls (*kunḍals*) prepared from feathers of birds. The curls were prepared so skillfully that they looked exactly natural hairs. On the auspicious occasion of Lohri festival in Chamba, people prepare a *hār* (garland) and *janjeeri* (chain) by sewing in a thread dry fruits such as cashewnuts, coconuts, chestnuts, peanuts, currant and pistachio, etc. in beautiful designs. The huge garland is worn by the youngest male in the family around the neck, while *janjeeri* is worn on the forehead by the female child.

The jewellery of Himalayan women consisted mainly of silver, as gold has been a rare and precious metal. There are ornaments which are for special occasions and there are ornaments meant for daily use. The love of Hindu women for ornaments is well known. It is a symbol of her status, it is her *stri-dhan* and a sign of *sohag* (married bliss), which no Indian law or custom can lay its hands on. The women, of course, wear jewellery profusely and, during the festivals of marriage they bring out all their jewellery and decorate themselves with it from head to toe. She will never accept parting from it. It is only in death that she is denuded of her jewellery. A dying person is stripped of jewellery, a widow is denuded of all her jewellery at the death of her husband and this marks the end of her joy, and, a negation of life itself. In this region we find depicted in old sculptures, on paintings and on *rumāl* the scenes from Indian epics, wherein men and women are shown wearing elaborate ornaments.

Adorning the person with jewellery starts from the birth of a child. A new born baby in the family is adorned with some ornaments like anklet made of *asṭh-dhatu*, silver or brass locally called *rehāḍu* or *ghungrālu*, and wristlets of silver *kangṇū*. It is said that the *rehāḍu* are worn to ward off the evil eye and to prevent the children from crying. They are made by the members of a menial caste named Rehāḍā. After passage of one year a *ṭdāgi* is worn around the waist of a male child which may be made of gold or silver depending upon the economic status of the family. In order to ward off the evil eyes and witchcraft a young boy is made to wear *nazar-baṭṭu* or *kunḍhu*. It is made of tooth and claw of a lion or a panther known as *bāgh-nakh*, encased in silver. In certain areas the small black seed of a soapnut is half encased in silver sheet with an oval hook at the centre. It is then tied with black thread and is worn around the neck. Besides this, on the day of the name-giving ceremony, the ears of the young one are pierced and golden ear rings, *murki*, decorated with beads, are worn in his ears. This ceremony is called *karaṇ-vedha*. The young girls get their nose also pierced and a *phulli, kokā*, or *murki* are put into them. Later on at the time of marriage a bride is given in dowry all the necessary ornaments by her parents, and her in-laws also present ornaments to her. Sometimes when the family has lost an infant, they pierce the nose of the male child and put a ring in it so that cruel nature should be misled into thinking that it is a girl child.

The love of Chamba women and men for ornaments is so great that even many of them get their teeth embossed with dots of gold called *phulli* or have their tooth encased in gold. There are also certain superstitions associated with gold. To pass gold from hand to hand or to loose gold or to find it are considered as bad omens and are said to lead to quarrels. Gold to many is a sacred metal and some swear by their gold rings by touching them. It is believed that the women's love of jewellery was not only for self-beautification but also out of necessity as they could change it for cash in times of need and adversity.

Lakshna Devi image of Brahmour (7th century A.D.) is wearing a kind of *dināramālā,* a necklace made of gold coins which was termed as '*nishka*' in the Vedas and other related ancient Hindu texts. Locally this necklace is termed as *hamail* or *mhail* and seems to be of hoary antiquity. The same kind of necklace is also worn by Śakti Devi image of Chhatrāḍi and Ganeśa image of Brahmour. The *dināramālā* seems to have been discontinued in the sculptural representation of Chamba but the tribal womenfolk especially Gujjars adhered to it and continued to wear this kind of *mālā* till today. *Hansli* is an ancient ornament and there are many sculptural representations of this ornament. Śakti Devi image of Chhatrāḍi (7th century A.D.) is seen wearing one. Another iconographical trait of the sculptures of Chamba is a sequence of bangles worn at the wrists by the female divinities. Possibly, this series of bangles was later on transformed into *ṭokās* or *bajuband* and can still be seen worn by womenfolk of Chamba. Many portraits in Pahāḍi style of the hill Rajas and nobels show them wearing pearl-studded *nantis* or ear-rings, while with the Mughal nobles this was not the case.

9

Ornaments for Head, Ears, Nose and Neck

1. Ornaments for Head

The main ornament for the head is *chouk* or *chaunk* or *chak*. It is a dome-like object resembling a Buddhist stupa or a dome. It looks like a miniature crown, and rightly deserves a place on the top of the head. *Chaunk* is of two kinds, one is a *sādā* or simple *chaunk* with a low hemispherical mound, and the other as the name suggests is an *uchā-chaunk,* i.e. a high *chaunk*. The upper class women of Chamba can afford the luxury of a gold *chaunk*, while the rest go for a silver one. The dome-shaped ornament has a small oval hook at the centre of the inner surface. Through this oval link a multicoloured thread *ḍori* is passed and the ornament is then secured to the locks of hair on the head. The *chaunk* is usually embossed with intricate designs and patterns. The floral work is generally carved out in one or two horizontal circles encased with lines of dots and dashes given in some symmetrical manner. The entire work has a harmony. The centre top of about 1 to 1.5 cms diameter is made more convex and forms a star shape. Diameter of average *chaunk* is about 8 cms, and height about 5 to 10 cms. Average weight of a *chaunk* comes to 60 to 150 grams. The top of a *chaunk* has a small neck, a sort of a bezel box, which is studded with a blue, red or dark green stone known as '*thewā*'. *Chaunk-boronwālā* or *laḍidār-chaunk* has small *jhumkās* with silver chains attached to it. The main accessory of a *chaunk* are two ornaments worn just over the ears and attached to the main *chaunk* by means of silver chains. They are called *phul* or *phullu*. This type of ornament is worn by the Gaddans, while the Chambyālans wear *phuls* (two *phuls*) only without attaching them to *chaunk* or *chouk* or *chak*. The *phul* are approximately 1/3rd of the *chaunk*. The entire arrangement of affixing *chaunk* and *phul* on the top and at the sides of head seems to be the relic of those ancient days when the hill women used to fix flowers in their hair for beautification.

Another prominent ornament of the head, rather forehead, is a *singārpaṭṭi (shringār-paṭṭi)*. *Singārpaṭṭi,* as the name suggests, is a plait-like ornament. On either ends of *singārpaṭṭi* are two hooks through which multi-coloured threads are passed for the purpose of tying it by giving it a knot at the back of the head. *Singārpaṭṭi*, like any other ornament, is made of either gold or silver. It is a broad strip of two knitted chains fringed with globular gold or silver beads and delicately worked 'pipal leaves'. Sometimes it is made of rectangular plaques linked to each other in a row. It weighs 20 to 25 grams. From *singārpaṭṭi* are hung innumerable *jhumkās*. They produce jingling sound at the slight movement of head. Large *jhumkās* or *karaṇphul* are hooked to each end of the *singārpaṭṭi*. They are then worn on the lobes of the ears. At the centre of *singārpaṭṭi* is fixed a disc-like ornament known as *manṭikkā*. This entire set of ornaments is then called *jhaṭpaṭṭu*. *Jhaṭpaṭṭu* is named as *janjeer* in Brahmour and *sirphool* by Gurkhas.

When *singārpaṭṭi* of silver has a central pendent either in the form of a half moon or full moon or a lotus flower with '*ghuṇgrus*' or 'pipal' leaves suspended from it, then it is called *chiḍi*. The disc of *chiḍi* is decorated with *meenā* work and is made of silver. This rests at the centre of the forehead. It weighs about 150 to 200 grams.

Manṭikkā or *mangṭikkā* or *ṭikkā* consists of a large circular disc, which comes right over the forehead. Sometimes it is hooked to *singārpaṭṭi* by means of a chain. The surface of this circular-shaped disc is engraved with floral motifs. The pipal leaves are suspended from the lower half of the disc. The ladies of Chamba

B1. Feathers made as decorative curls, *kuṇḍals*, for fastening to the hair.

B2. Nitika wearing ornaments of dry fruits for Lohri festival.

B3. String having beads which ward off evil eye called *nazar-baṭṭu* or *kuṇḍhu*.

B4. Head ornament which is braided in hair known as *chaunk* and *phull*.

B5. Plait to be worn over combed hair above the forehead called *singārpaṭṭi*.

B6. Round forehead ornament known as *chiḍi*.

B7. Forehead ornament *chiḍi* fastend to hair plait, *singārpaṭṭi*.

B8. Round forehead ornament known as *chilkainwala manṭikā*.

B9. Crescent-shaped forehead ornament called *argh-chandru*.

B10. Chain called *janjeer* or *shangli*.

B11. Ear ring known as *bāle*.

B12. Ear rings which are put arround the ear called *kālu* or *kāḍu*.

B13. Flower-shaped ear stud fastened to hair with chain called *karaṇ-phul*, suspended lobe attached to the *karaṇ-phul* makes it a pair of *lurku*.

B14. Big round ear stud called *pharālu*.

B15. Cap-shaped ear ornament called *jhumkā*.

B16. Prominent nose ring called *Bālu*.

B17. Nose ring, central piece is made by joining five pipal leaves known as *chutkiwālā bālu*.

B18. Ornament which is suspended from the septum of the nose called *balākḍu* or *ḍoḍā-balāk*.

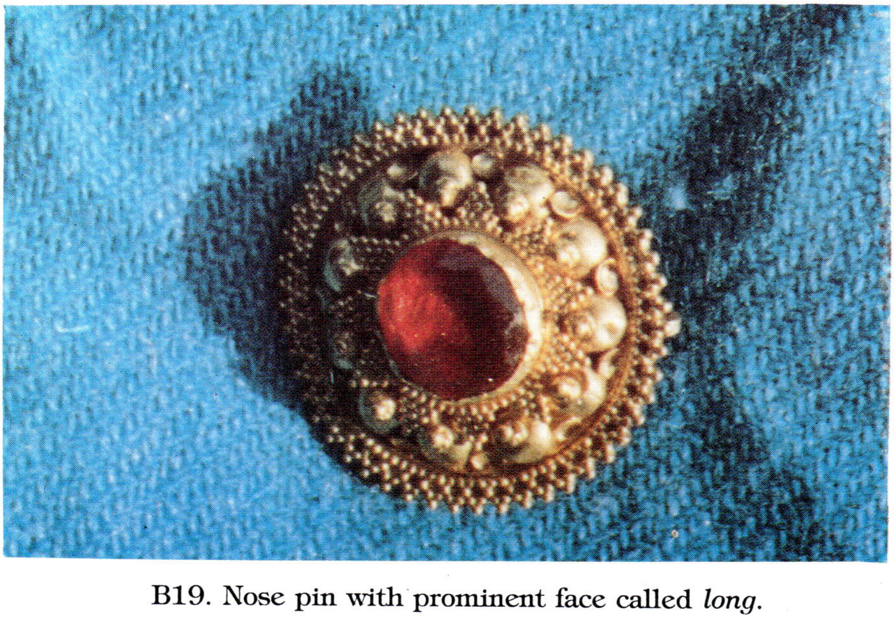

B19. Nose pin with prominent face called *long*.

B20. Ring which is suspended from the septum of nose called *nathli*.

B21. Necklace which has bud-like pieces strung in the thread called *chamkali* or *jaumālā* (Courtesy Bhuri Singh Museum, Chamba).

B22. Necklace which has round piece like soapnut called *ḍoḍmālā*.

B23. Ornament having three rows of small beads worn tightly on the neck called *kanṭhṇu*.

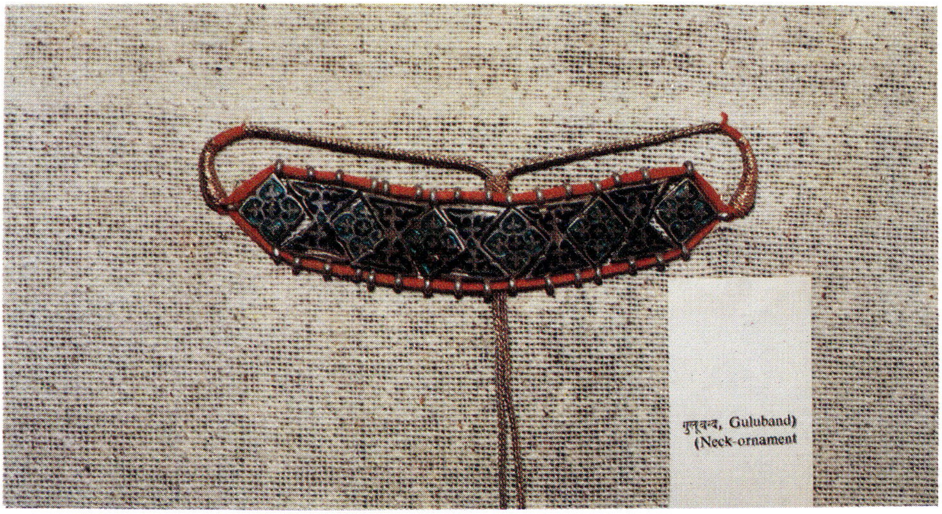

B24. Broad strip meant for decorating the neck, made up by joining enamelled pieces with hooks to parallel threads known as *gulband* or *guluband* (Courtesy Bhuri Singh Museum, Chamba).

B25. Heart or leaf-shaped or a round pendant which is fitted with coloured stones called *nām*.

B26. Necklace with square pendant containing a painting of Śiva *parivār* called *sabihi* (Courtesy Bhuri Singh Museum, Chamba).

B27. Squar pendant known as *tabeet*.

B28. The *chanderhār* to be worn in neck.

B29. Sickle-shaped neck ornament called *hansli* or *sahiri*.

B30. Necklace in which old coins are strung to the thread called *mhail* or *hamail*.

B31. Small pendant having figures of deceased person called *auttar*.

B32. A cylindrical hallow capsule made into a pendant by means of hooks called *ḍhol* or *dhadi*.

B33. Bangle for the upper arm called *nant*.

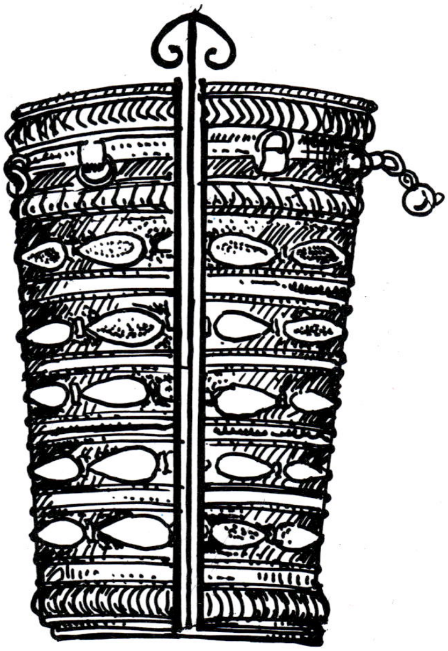

B34. Broad wrist ornament called *bajuband*.

B35. Heavy bracelets having lion head-ends called *kangṇū.*

B36. A variation of *kangṇū* known as *gokhru*.

B37. Hollowed bangles known as *maredaḍi* or *gōjru*.

B38. Wrist bangles, gold bar is interlaced and ends have lion-mouth called *kangṇū* (*kangaṇ*).

B39. A type of designed bangles called *ṭoke*.

B40. Wrist bangles provided with jingling *bores* called *chhaṇ-kangaṇ.*

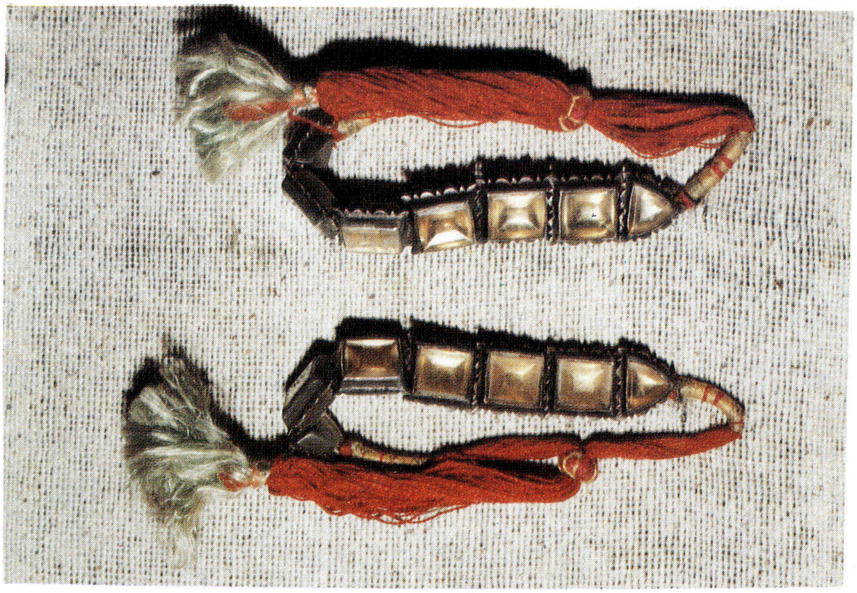

B41. Wrist strap called *ponchhi* (Courtesy Bhuri Singh Museum, Chamba).

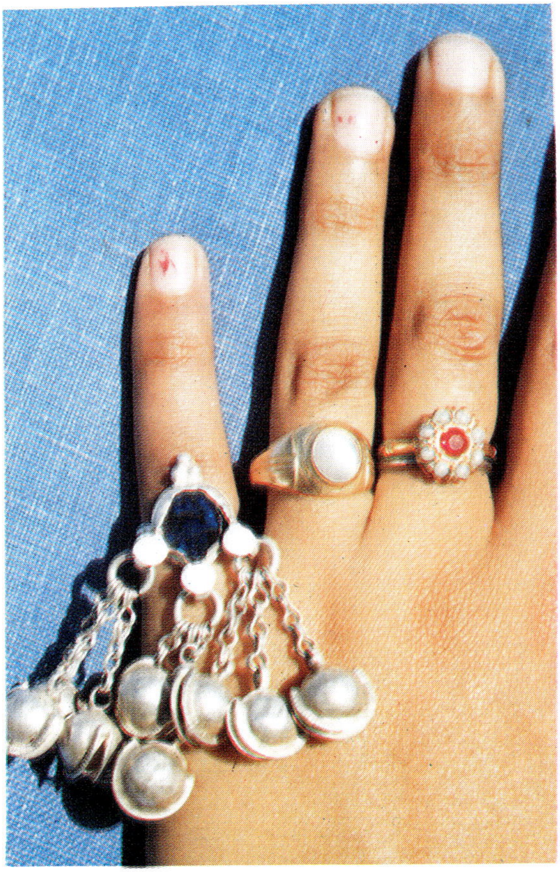

B42. Finger rings in different designs.

B43. Ring for the thumb with a mirror called *arsi*.

B44. Ornament for fore-finger called *nahastrā*. (Courtesy Bhuri Singh Museum, Chamba).

B45. A popular ankle ornament with cluster of jingling balls called *panjeb*.

B46. Delicately designed ankle ornament called *toḍā*.

B47. Hollowed and designed ankle ornament called *jhānjhar.*

B48. Toe ring called *porḍi.*

B49. Silver buttons and chain.

B50. Three-stringed *mālā* of silver beads.

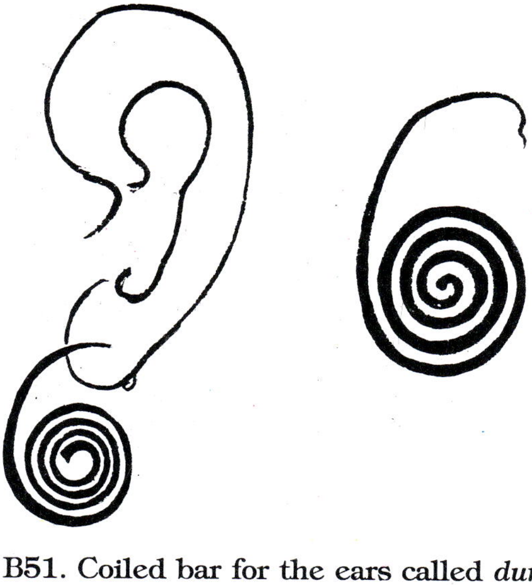

B51. Coiled bar for the ears called *dur*.

B52. Scent box called *attar-dāni*.

B53. Horse hair bangles and finger rings (Courtesy Bhuri Singh Museum, Chamba).

B54. An elderly Gujjar woman wearing a traditional jewellery.

town and village belles are seen wearing it. The diameter of the plaque varies from 5 to 6 cms and weighs about 15 to 50 grams. It is prepared in gold and displays a number of designs. To the lower edge of the plaque a bunch of gold leaves or rounded beads are attached.

Another type of *manṭikkā* which is also in vogue, is in the shape of crescent moon, and is called *argh-chandru* or *chandru* (*ardh-chandra*), meaning half moon. On this crescent shape is affixed either one cut-piece of *chuni* stone covering the entire crescent, or the surface is decorated with the motifs of flower, rosettes or with blue, white or red imitation stones of diamond shape. The circular edge of the *argh-chandru* is affixed with rounded beads. It is generally worn on the right side of the forehead. *Argh-chandru* is smaller in size and it is prepared from gold. It weighs about 5 to 8 grams.

Another ornament common in use is a sort of hair-clip prepared locally. It is meant for keeping the arrangement of the hair in order and is like any other ordinary clip available in the market. It is made either of gold or of silver. It is approximately 6 to 7 cms long and 1.5 to 2 cms wide and weighs about 1 to 5 grams. On its back a pin and a hook is provided by which it is fixed to the hair. With the advent of innumerable varieties of plastic and other kinds of fancy clips, this kind of ornament is also becoming extinct.

Another ornament which resembles *singārpaṭṭi* is called *janjeer* or *shangli* and is a peculiar head ornament of Churāhans of upper Churāh tehsil. It is attached to the *joji* and fastened to the hair above the ears on one side. It gives a dashing and seductive look. It consists of a broad band, which is knitted together by silver wire, and is about 20 to 25 cms long. In between the knitted plait are seen four bezel boxes, which are studded with coloured imitation stones.

Sometimes it is prepared of three or four knitted silver chains, which are attached by hooks at both ends. The pipal leaves are suspended to the bottom chain.

Another ornament of head, which seems to be an import from the plains is *jhumar. Jhumar* consists of a bunch of round jingling beads, which are hung together by means of silver chains over the right side of the forehead and is fixed with the help of a hook in the hair. It is no longer in vogue except with the women of Bhaṭṭiyāt.

2. Ornaments for Ears

Ornaments for ears range from a simple and small *tilli* to highly intricate designs of *phair* and *bālies*. The ornaments for the ears consist of *bāle, bāli, phair, kālū, kānṭe* and *bunḍe* etc. The simplest ornament is *tilli*, which weighs only a few grams and is thin like match stick but not more than a centimetre in length. It has a silver or gold knob at one end. Sometimes the knob of *tilli* is decorated with different designs. The *tilli* is worn mostly by the women of Pāngi and upper Churāh. In Chamba the *tilli* is made of gold and instead of knob it has a bezel box, which is studded with an imitation stone.

Bāle or *phair* is the main ornament of the ears. Its shape is like that of an ear ring but with a beautiful decorative work done on it. The *bāle* is made of a molded silver or gold coil around which runs a thin silver or gold wire in spiral form. An embossed metal of crescent shape is fitted to the wire by a hinge at one end, and a hook on the other. The lower edge is extended with the wire work carrying flat or round pieces of metals fixed at regular intervals. From this small round beads or bunches of 'pipal' leaves are suspended. A pair of *bāle* normally weighs about 15 to 30 grams. It is normally worn on lobes of the ears. With slight improvisation it is worn by Gujjar women and is called *gol*. A small version of *bāle* is called *bāli* or *chhiku*. In Chamba town there has also been a tradition of wearing a plain gold ring without any ornamental work done on it.

The women from Pāngi and the upper Churāh have the custom

of wearing 10 to 12 rings in the lobes of the ears at a stretch. All these ear rings are called *kālu* or *kāḍu* in local dialects. These rings are encircled with silver wire and weigh about 2 to 3 grams. The Gurkha women also wear a kind of *bāles* which they call *mārūḍi*. This ear ring has a gold flap at the dangling end and is decorated with the motifs of flower petals and rosettes.

Names such as *pharālu, jhumku (jhumkā), karaṇ-phul (phulu), kan-chhiku* and *ḍeḍku* signify the same ornament for the ears, but different names are applied in different localities and also the shape of the ornament slightly varies from region to region. *Pharālu* is an ear stud usually covering the lobes of the ears. It is either enamelled or chased round stud, sometimes filled with turquoise in the centre. Its outer edge resembles a star and is sometimes imbedded with a wire ring giving the impression of joined knobs. *Jhumkā* is a dome-shaped ornament having a number of small bunches of rounded beads hanging from it. When the *karaṇ-phul* is fitted with a stone *sabzā*, then it is called *lurka*. Another variety of it is named *ḍeḍku* (*ḍhoḍku*), when it is provided with a hook to dangle it from the ears. A pair of these ornaments weighs about 15 to 30 grams and is about 4 to 5 cms long.

Sāngli with *jhumku* means a pair of *jhumkās* with a long chain in between. The chain is passed behind the ear, then temporal portion of the head and brought around the front portion of the ears and the *jhumkās* attached to it by means of hooks are suspended from the lobes. The popular shape of *jhumku* consists of dome-like shape with intricate designs, and several *jhumkās* are suspended from it by means of a tiny chain.

The *sānkali* is prevalent mostly in upper Churāh and Pāngi tehsils. In Pāngi it is pronounced as '*sangḍi*'. *Sānkali* as the name suggests is nothing but a pair of long chain suspended from the lobe of each ear and hanging over the breast. A pair of *sānkali* weighs about 30 to 40 grams.

Another ornament of the ear is called *kānṭā*. This ear ring is made in several geometrical designs and is about 4 to 6 cms long. Usually it is suspended from the lobes of the ears, has a dome-like shape, from which hang by means of small chains numerous beads or studded stones. This is the popular shape of the ornament. The long *kāṇṭā* is provided with a thin long chain which is drawn around the ear. The ornament is prepared in gold and silver and each pair weighs 5 to 15 grams.

Buṇḍe as the name implies consists of a small circular disc decorated with numerous dots (*buṇḍe*) in various designs. It is held to the ear by means of a hook. Mostly it is made of silver and weighs hardly a few grams.

Ṭops resemble *buṇḍe*. This ornament consists of two parts which are held together by means of a screw. It weighs only a few grams. The knob of the *ṭops* is circular in shape and decorated with one major imitation stone at the centre and with minor or small stones all around. We have described here only the popular design, but the *ṭops* can be prepared in any shape or design according to the whims and fancy of the lady wearing it.

3. Ornaments for Nose

The main ornaments of the nose are *bālu*, and *besār*. It attracts attention at once, because it is worn over the face itself. It provides shine and glow and a sense of mystery to the woman wearing it. The glitter and the dazzle of *bālu* holds the attention of the beholder towards the lovely face of the woman. There is hardly a Pahāḍi (Kangra) painting in which a feminine beauty is shown without adorning a *bālu*. *Bālu* is worn at the right side of the nose and it comes over the cheek. A long chain is fixed somewhere in the hairs and helps in keeping it at place. The chain is a necessary accessory as the *bālu* is heavy to wear. The lady has either to remove it entirely or to lift it upwards with one hand to keep the way to the mouth open while eating. *Bālu* is worn by almost all the women of Chamba district except for the ladies of Pāngi and upper

Churāh. The shape of the *bālu* is like a large ring. The *bālu* is of many kinds. The *sādā bālu*, which is worn by the ladies of Brahmour, is a plain *bālu* with three or four small circular discs, *ṭikis*, studded with pearls which are connected to the ring of *bālu*. It weighs about 15 to 20 grams and is made of gold.

Another kind of *bālu* is called *chuṭkiwālā bālu*. It is a *bālu*, the inside of which is decorated with a *chuṭki*. The word *chuṭki* denotes a thing insignificantly small (like a pinch of something), thus *chuṭki* is a small decorative motif which is attached to the ring of *bālu*. In other words, in a *sādā bālu* the inner space in the *bālu* is empty, while in *chuṭkiwālā bālu*, a small space is decorated with *chuṭki*, i.e. a decorative design. *Jaḍāu bālu* unlike the other *bālus* consists of a crescent-shaped ring which is studded with various kinds of imitation stones, and the ring is completed with a simple wire to put it into the nose. In addition, it has also a *chuṭki* inset with imitation stones.

Another kind of *bālu* is a *besār* in which a bird motif is shown setting on the ring. Sometimes a floral motif replaces the bird motif. These types of *bālus* are quite heavy ornaments, and weigh about 30 to 40 grams. These are made solid and are prepared in gold. The diameter of the ring is roughly 8 to 10 cms.

Nath is another ornament like *bālu* or *besār*. The ornament is popular one and is a familiar name throughout India. Curiously it has been associated with the virginity of a woman, though not in Himachal Pradesh, yet here also it has some link with the matrimony, as a newly married woman is supposed to wear a *nath* for a year or so. There are many songs prevalent in this region as well as in Rajasthan and other parts of India associated with the beauty of a *nath*. *Nath* is a *bālu* in miniature. Probably women found it cumbersome to wear *bālu* all the times, hence the need for something smaller might have been felt which could be worn daily and which would not come in the way of taking food. Now urbanised women as well as the tribal women no longer wear it daily. But it is certainly a necessary item of their jewellery box.

During the fairs and festivals and marriage ceremonies women of Chamba take pride in wearing this exotic ornament. The festival of 'Karwā-Chauth' is gaining popularity in Chamba and in this festival there is hardly a married woman who is seen without a *bālu, nath* and *besār. Nath* and *bālu* in Chamba are also associated with *suhāg* (married bliss—long life of the husband) since long times. It is used so long as the husband is alive. The gold ring of *nath* here is smaller in size and carries a simple design. Sometimes it is made of thin wire with only a hook and no decoration. The *nath* is always made of gold and weighs 15 to 25 grams or even less.

On seeing *bulāk or balāk* one is at once reminded of padlock. To wear this ornament a woman should have a hole pierced in the septum of her nostrils. The perforation is done in the childhood. It is held suspended over the lips and is in the shape of a hollowed 'pipal' leaf. A *chhilkāwāli balāk* has small *chhilkās,* i.e. small 'pipal' leaves attached to it. A *balākḍu* or *ḍoḍā balāk* is a mini *balāk* having small drops all around it. The weight of *balāk* is about 8 to 12 grams and *balākḍu* is 3 to 4 grams. The *balāk* has now become obscure, but the ladies of some villages in Churāh, Brahmour and Pāngi tehsils continue to wear it even today.

Tilli is a very popular ornament throughout the region. It is thin pin like a straw and weighs only a few grams. It is the simplest and the lightest of all the ornaments. Probably it is reminiscent of those ancient days when a tribal woman used to insert a tiny and very thin piece of straw into her nose. Curiously many tribal women are still seen wearing *tilli* made of straw. The name *tilli* itself suggests that previously it used to be a mere piece of straw. Many women of Chamba invariably use it for insertion after getting their nose and ears pierced. They prefer it as the skin is raw at that time and unable to bear the touch of a hard metal. Some imaginative belle go in for a flower to enchant her suitor. Now the *tilli* is made either of gold or silver, and can be got prepared in different shapes and designs. *Tillis* are also mechanically prepared and the fancy shops are full of it.

A variation of *tilli* is *kokā* which weighs less than half a gram. The *kokā* is like a small nail. It is prepared in gold and the nail head is sometimes studded with red stone known as *thewa*. It is fitted inside the nose by means of a *koli*, a sort of an empty case.

Another ornament *phulli* is worn in the nose like *tilli* or *kokā*. But it is slightly different in design. Now here on the knob-head is carved a star-shaped motif studded in centre with an imitation stone surrounded by minor jewels. It weighs about a gram and is made of gold or silver.

Long unlike *tilli, phulli* and *kokā* is a major ornament of the nose. It is prepared from gold and weighs about 3 to 6 grams. Here the knob or the nail-head has the diameter of a fifty paise coin, on which a convexed round disc is soldered. On its surface grain work is done. Sometimes a small flat red jewel known as *nag* is fitted in the bezel box provided in the centre. On the reverse of this ornament a hallowed pin is fixed and inserted into the right side of the nose. This ornament is popular throughout the region.

Another range of nose ornaments bear the names of *kuṇḍā* (*kuṇḍi*), *murki* and *nathli*. These ornaments are fixed in the septum of the nose and are made to hang over the upper lip. A *kuṇḍā* or *kuṇḍi* is a gold ring but without any decoration. The average diameter of *kuṇḍā* is roughly 1.50 to 3 cms, and it weighs anywhere between one to two grams. The *nathli* or *murki* is another variety of the nose ornament. *Kuṇḍā* is a plain gold ring but it is attached with a decorative disc which increases its size so that it reaches even upto the lower lip. The disc is studded with sparkling red stones at the centre but the rest of the portion is finely executed with grain work. The *murki* is always made of gold. It may have different sizes, shapes and designs. The weight of the *murki* varies from 3 to 4 grams. When the weight is more than 4 grams, they are named as *nathli*. Some *murkis* and *nathlis* are in the form of a triangle while others are betel-shaped. At its upper portion a hinge and a hook are provided, wherein a carved wire is fixed by which it is hung to the septum of the nose.

Another ornament of the nose is *ṭiki* and, as the name connotes, it is a flat, circular plaque worn at the right side of the nose. It weighs about one gram and is always prepared in gold.

4. Ornaments for Neck

The prominent necklace common in Chamba district is *chamkali (champākali)* or *jau-mālā*. The *chamkali* derives its name from *champākali* and resembles the buds of *champak* flower (*Michelia champaka*). In some regions of this area *chamkali* or *champākali* is named as *jau-mālā*. *Jau-mālā* differs from *chamkali* only in its small size and its buds resemble the shoots. In *chamkali* or *champākali* and *jau-mālā* several pieces of *champak* and *jau* (barley) shaped silver buds are strewn to form a single necklace. The silver buds are hollowed from inside and sometimes a thin silver sheet is cut into several pieces in the shape of buds. A necklace weighs about 50 grams and has about 30 to 40 buds. Very rarely the silver leaves thus strung together to form a necklace have small bunches of hollowed pipal leaves or *jhumkās* attached to it.

Ḍoḍ-mālā is prepared from the beads resembling soapnut, *ḍoḍā*. It is possible that in ancient times, when the human beings used to decorate themselves with fresh flowers, fruits etc., they might have also prepared a garland of soapnuts. The soapnuts produce a rumbling sound and the garland must have been a popular one. *Ḍoḍ-mālā* is prepared by means of hollowed round silver balls approximating the size of a soapnut. Two half portions of a bead are prepared by stamping a silver sheet on a mould called *ḍoḍ-mālā-ki-mosh*. Then both the units are soldered at the edges, leaving a hole at the ends. The beads are then threaded with a cotton thread. Usually a *ḍoḍ-mālā* is a two to three-stringed necklace, but the two-stringed *ḍoḍ-mālā* is common. At each end of the necklace a betel-shaped or a triangular plaque is provided which holds the strings of *ḍoḍ-mālā* together. Each of these plaques has a small twisted thread by which the necklace is tied at the back of the neck. Normally each string of necklace carries twenty-five to thirty beads. It weighs 120 to 180 grams. This type of necklace is very popular throughout the district, even the men wear a *ḍoḍ-mālā* once in a while.

Galsāri or *galsri* or *gulband* is another ornament for the decoration of neck. This ornament is worn quite close to the neck. It is about 15 to 20 cms long and about 2 to 3 cms wide and weighs about 30 to 50 grams. It consists of several rows of parallel beaded strings. The strings are held together at the two ends by triangular plaques. This type of *galsāri* is also known by the name of *kanṭhṇu.* Another kind of *galsāri* is made of a number of rectangular plaques of silver linked to each other and decorated with *meenā* work. It is also worn close to the neck and is provided with a coloured thread for tying it at the back of the neck. This type of ornament is called *galpāṭṭu* in Pāngi.

The *nām* is a heart-shaped or a betel-shaped or a circular pendant coming right in between the two breasts. The pendant is provided with hooks, through which a multi-coloured twisted thread is passed to form a necklace. The pendant is decorated with several engraved figural and floral designs. This betel-shaped pendant has usually two or three different borders decorated with different designs. An oval imitation stone, *sabzā* or a bud made of gold is suspended from its apex which shakes to and fro at the slightest movement. The ornament is made of gold and weighs 10 to 25 grams.

Kanṭhā is another necklace for the adornation of the neck. Like *nām* it has a circular pendant suspended from the neck by means of a string, which is threaded with beads of the same metal. It is usually made of gold and weighs 50 grams. In Pāngi it is called *kanṭhḍu.*

Sabihi or *Sabhi* is another ornament which is very enchanting to look at and is worn throughout the region. The *sabihi,* though a Persian-sounding word, is derived from the Hindi word 'Chhavi', which means a portrait or a painting. True to its name the *sabihi* consists of a large square or rectangular frame, a silver case, on which is fixed a painting with religious theme and then a glass panel is set over it. In short the *sabihi* is a painting framed in a silver case. The *sabihi* is suspended from four or five rings attached to the upper part of the frame, through which a multi-coloured thread is passed. These rings are affixed with circular discs for decoration. A *sabihi* often has few bunches of *jhumkās* suspended from its lower portion. Sometimes round circular discs are attached at the lower portion. Its weight is about 200 to 250 grams.

A *sabihi*-like ornament is worn by both the males and females of Gujjar tribe which is called a *tabeet. Tabeet* seems to be the distortion of *tabeez*, which was worn and is still worn as a magic amulet to ward off evil spirits. *Tabeet* is an ornament smaller in shape and simpler in design. It is a thin rectangular piece of silver embossed with floral or figural work. It has two or four hooks and is suspended from the neck by means of a multi-coloured thread which passes through the hooks. Globular beads are suspended from *tabeet* by means of small chains. Sometimes instead of the embossed work, a dark blue coloured glass is fixed covering the entire surface of the silver plaque. It weighs 250 grams. The Gaddi men also wear it.

Pendal (derivative of English pendant) is a modern ornament and consists of a small circular pendant studded with an imitation stone of any colour. It is hooked with a golden or silver chain, which gives it the shape of a necklace. In short the *pendal* is made of a pendant and a chain. It weighs from 6 to 12 grams.

The major ornament for the neck is *satlaḍi-hār*. The number seven is considered to be an auspicious one in Hindu religion. The *satlaḍi-hār* is a seven-stringed necklace made of circular flower rosettes. When these chains are combined with large enamelled plaques or embossed with plaques carrying geometrical patterns then it is called *chandar-hār* or *gunj*. These chains end in triangular plaques decorated with floral and figural motifs. Attached with these plaques are three or four silver chains which cover the back portion of the neck when the necklace is worn. The *chandar-hār* or *gunj* as it is called in Chamba town is made of a five or seven strings with the square pendant at the centre of a necklace and two other smaller square plaques set on either side. In Bakloh area of Bhaṭṭiyāt tehsil, *gunj* is worn by Gurkha women and is called *teep-mālā*. There the *teep-mālā* is tied to the neck by means of very fine twisted golden or silken threads. *Gunj* and *teep-mālā* are made in gold, whereas *satlaḍi-hār* and *chandar-hār* are silver ornaments. The ornament is about 200 grams in weight and its length is about 30 to 35 cms. *Satlaḍi-hār* is also called *rani-hār*, when certain modifications are made to it, but the basic form remains the same.

Til-hār is a *mangal-sutra* worn by Gurkha women. It is prepared from small black round beads threaded together in the form of necklace. At the centre of the necklace hangs a circular pendant made of gold which is ornamented with floral motifs. Its weight is 6 to 10 grams.

Mālā is a simple necklace made of beads of gold or silver, linked to each other by means of a wire. It weights about 15 to 20 grams.

Hansli, hanseeri or *sahiri* is fashioned in the form of a sickle or a *hansli*. It has no loose parts and is made out of broad silver sheet, which is moulded in the shape of a crescent. Its two ends are shaped in the form of a round knob. The central portion of *hansli* is comparatively thick and carries various designs. Sometimes, it is shaped exactly like a sickle excluding handle, and is as sharp and thin as a sickle. The circumference of a *hansli* may be 38 to 50 cms and it weighs about 150 to 250 grams. *Boron-wāli hansli* has few round hollowed balls attached to it. This ornament is popular with the Gujjars. It is said that earlier it was also worn by Gujjar males. The heavy silver neck-rings (*hansli*) also seems to be of Central Asian origin.[1]

1. Hermann Goetz, *Art and Architecture of Bikaner State*, Oxford (1950), p. 121.

Butki or *bugdī* is a necklace made of discs of gold, shaped like coins which are stamped with designs. When this ornament is prepared in silver it is called *dussar*. Usually *bugdī* is composed of 8 to 12 discs and each disc weighs about 5 to 10 grams.

Mhail or *hamail* necklace is made of coins. This necklace is much in vogue in the Gujjar community. In Brahmour this necklace is called *kanḍhu*. Old silver coins of four and eight annas and of a rupee denomination are used to make this ornament. The coin is soldered at the border with a ring through which twisted thread is passed, which gives it a form of a necklace. Normally coins which are uniform and of the same denomination are used. Sometimes in the centre a big heart-shaped leaf or a plaque of silver with embossed work is suspended. The ornament weighs about 100 to 150 grams. According to Dr. Bhandarkar such necklaces in the Jaina Kalpa Sutra were called 'Uratha-dināra-mālāya', i.e. a string of dinars (Persian gold coin) on the breast (as stated earlier).

Auttar is another ornament worn by the tribal women. When a male member in the family dies issueless, he is believed to take the form of a ghost according to the local tradition, and gives trouble to the members of the family. To ward off his evil designs a sort of magic amulet is embossed with the effigy of the dead male member (*auter*) on a rectangular or a triangular plaque of silver, which is then worn around the neck by means of twisted black thread. It weighs 2 to 3 grams. *Auttars* are also said to have been admitted into the category of the deities owing to their influence on men and women. The word is derived from the Sanskrit word, *āputtar,* a man having died without issue. Their spirits are also propitiated on the days of *amāvas* and *puranmāshi*.

Nādi or *singi* resembles the shape of a hollow reed or an hour-glass. It also recalls to mind the drum of Śiva (*damru*), except that it is hollowed from inside and one can look from one end of *singi* to the other. The Gaddis or the followers of Nāth sect wear it as an auspicious sign of Śiva. The *singi* is compressed at the centre and on this narrow portion a ring is attached through which a thread is passed for the purpose of hanging it from the neck. It weighs about 8 to 15 grams of silver or gold and its length is about 3 to 8 cms with varying thickness. Sometimes bunches of drops are also hung from it, and is known as *rālū*. It is worn both by males and females.

Jantar is a small rectangular case of silver, copper or gold in which is deposited a Talisman or 'Yantra' drawn on paper to keep off ill effects of witches. About 5 grams of silver or gold is sufficient to make the case. The copper *jantars* are bought readymade from the market. An oval hook is soldered on the upper edge, and a black twisted thread is passed through this hook to form a necklace. *Jantar* is worn both by men and women and even by small children.

Ḍhaḍi or *ḍhol* is an air-tight hollowed capsule-shaped silver ornament. Although it resembles a charm but nothing is kept inside. It is a sort of hollowed drum (*ḍhol*), 5 cms long and 2 cms thick. For dangling it in front of the neck two hooks are soldered to it through which the black twisted thread is passed. The body of the *ḍhol* carries simple geometrical designs. It weighs about 25 grams. Sometimes a few clusters of drops (*bore*) are made to hang from it. Mostly Gaddis, Churāhīs and Gujjars wear it.

10

Ornaments for Upper Arms, Wrists and Fingers

1. Ornaments for Upper Arms

Nant (anant) is an armlet prepared by moulding the solid bar of silver or gold into a round shape. The two ends of the bar do not meet each other when worn over the upper arm but overlap each other thus clasping the arm firmly but without causing any irritation. This ornament is thicker at the centre. The *nant* has some connection with religious beliefs. The centre portion of *nant* is engraved with 14 auspicious symbols. The two ends of the *nant* are round like knobs. It weighs 12 to 15 grams.

Jantar is a small rectangular case of silver or copper, having two hooks on either sides. By opening the lid, a 'Yantra' or Talismān made on a piece of paper after magical recitations is placed. The paper is folded and wrapped with red coloured threads and then molten wax of bees is applied to it so that it becomes water-proof, and is not soiled, while taking bath. After placing in the Talismān paper the lid is put tightly over it. It is then tied around the upper arm with a black thread. It weighs 2.5 to 3 grams.

2. Ornaments for Wrists

The *bajuband* has a cylinder-like shape, which slightly tapers towards the lower end. This cylindrical shape is prepared out of two sheets of silver, each sheet constituting the one half of the ornament. These two round sheets are then joined together by means of hinges and this constitutes the entire *bajuband*. It is worn right over the wrist unlike bangles. A pin is required to close the two ends of *bajuband*. The body of the *bajuband* carries dotted designs all over it resembling cucumber seeds. *Bajuband* is 13 to 16 cms wide and perhaps it is the largest of all the ornaments for the wrist. A pair of it weighs about 250 to 300 grams of silver. This ornament is also named as *chuḍā* in some parts of the region.

Another type of *bajuband* comes in one piece and has no hinges or joints. The two ends of the *bajuband* do not meet each other. It is flexible and can be stretched for wearing over the wrist and then closed by slight pressure.

Kangṇū which is popular in Chamba is also known as *gokhrū*. *Kangṇū* is prepared by moulding solid bar of silver into a round shape of a bangle except that here the two ends do not meet and the open ends are shaped in the form of lions staring at each other. A sufficient space is left between the two heads of lions. On *gokhrū* the dents are cut in a line and the rounded bar is little flattened and separated in two parts by cutting a channel in the centre. Open ends of *gokhrū* have either *makra* or lion heads. A pair of it weighs about 250 to 400 grams. *Kangṇū* bearing lions' faces is also known *haroḍu* in Pāngi area. There it becomes a heavy ornament weighing about 700 to 800 grams. In Brahmour these *kangṇūs* appear in brass as *ghoḍoli* and are prepared by the Thaṭhiār or Rehāḍā (coppersmiths).

Maredaḍi or *gōjru* is a hollowed bangle. Its surface is covered all over with saw-teeth decoration. It has a hinge and can be pulled apart from the wrist. Its width is 3 cms. A pair of *maredaḍi* weighs about 150 to 200 grams.

Kangṇū comes in many other designs and varieties which are still popular in Chamba. Infants are made to wear a small ringlet made by twisting a simple plate of silver into a bangle shape. To the body of this ringlet are attached oval hooks through which are suspended numerous *bores* (hollowed balls of metal). This is the befitting ornament for the little ones for they cannot keep their hands still and the pleasant sound of these beads provides them with constant amusement. A busy house-wife absorbed in her household chores can always know by the sound of the jingling beads, the whereabout of her kid in the house, for the infants have a tendency of moving out of the house or playing at some corner in the house, which may be unsafe for them. The weight of a pair of these *kangṇū* is about 20 to 25 grams.

Another interesting *kangṇū (kangaṇ)* which is very popular in this region is in the shape of two interlacing snakes with the faces of lion at two ends. It is prepared both in silver and gold, and a pair of it weighs about 50 to 80 grams.

Ṭoke is prepared from a silver plate (width 4 cms, thickness 1/8 cm). This silver plate is rounded leaving a space of a few cms between the two ends. The upper surface of *ṭoke* is covered with the designs of hollowed cucumber seeds in rows. Usually there are two or four such rows. The inner surface of *ṭoke* is plain, shining and smooth. While the basic form of *ṭoke* remains the same as explained above, the body of *ṭoke* may carry different designs. The *ṭoke* is still one of the major wrist ornaments and the ladies love to wear it. When a cluster of *jhumkās* are attached to it, it becomes a *chhaṇ-kangaṇ*. In Brahmour this ornament is named as '*chhar-kangaṇ*'. The *ṭoke* are made of silver or gold, but *chhaṇ-kangaṇs* are always made of silver. A pair of *ṭoke* weighs between 120 and 250 grams.

Ponchhi has a shape of a metal strap of a wrist watch, and like the same it is strapped around the wrist. It is prepared by knitting together silver wires producing different designs and patterns. Sometimes the strip of a *ponchhi* is composed of a row of loosely fitted rectangular plaques carrying *meenā*-work or studded with stones. A pair of *ponchhi* weighs 80 to 100 grams and its width is about 3 cms.

The *bang* or the *chuḍi,* i.e. bangles, need no special comment as it is not prepared in any special way which could distinguish it from the similar ornament as worn in the rest of the state. Here mention may be made of *Borāwāli bang* i.e. a *bang* or a bangle attached with *bore* (hollowed beads or balls) which is peculiar to this region. Its weight is about 10 to 12 grams and the width is 1.5 to 2 cms.

3. Ornaments for Fingers

Arsi or *arsu* means a mirror. An ornament with this name is a ring fitted with a round mirror or a looking-glass. It is usually worn on the thumb of the right hand. With the help of *arsi*, the hill woman can look at herself in the mirror and feel assured of her beauty in such places like fairs and festivals. Thus she can stealthily have a glance in the mirror whenever she desires, even in the company of males without feeling awkward.

Arsi is prepared by insetting a round looking-glass on a large round silver frame having a decorative border. *Arsi* is then soldered to the ring for wearing on the thumb. This ornament is prepared both in silver and gold. The average diameter of *arsi* is 5 to 7 cms and its weight is about 50 to 70 grams. The ornament unfortunately is falling into disuse probably because of its large size and also because of change in the social status of women. When this ornament appears in smaller shape, it is called *arsu.*

Nahastrā is another form of ring having a triangular and pointed nail-like formation on it. *Nahastrā* seems to be the combination of two words *nah* + *astrā* (nail + weapon). This triangular space is decorated in various designs. Usually at the centre is set a large *pherozā* variety of stone. It weighs about 5 to 10 grams.

Chhallā is thin round strip of a silver and unlike ring it has three to four coils. The *chhallā* is coiled in spirals, hence two ends do not meet each other. It is generally worn in the little or ring fingers. Its weight is about 2 to 4 grams.

Ring is called *anguṭhi* or *mundri*. Usually it is thick in size showing two bezel boxes in which are set imitation stones of different colours. Sometimes the ring is attached to a broad strip of silver which is dotted with small blue and red imitation stones. Another popular gold *anguṭhi* consists of a large bezel box with a red bright imitation stone set in it. It may be prepared either in gold or in silver. The *mundri* of Gaddis, Pangwālās and Churāhīs is prepared of silver and is studded with *pherozā* stone. It weighs 5 to 10 grams.

11

Ornaments for Ankels and Toes, for Males, and other Decorative Pieces

1. Ornaments for Ankels

Pājeb is a Persian word meaning an ornament for the decoration of foot. In local dialect *pājeb* is termed as *panjeb*. This anklet is prepared by the mesh of interlacing silver wires. Innumerable jingling balls of silver are suspended from the hooks attached to its lower border. A pair of *panjeb* weighs about 350 to 500 grams. The width of *panjeb* is 3 to 4 cms. It is also believed that the sound of these jingling beads shies away the scorpions and snakes, which seems to be true to some extent. In a household where there are many women, each one of them may be identified merely from the sound of the *panjeb* worn by her.

Toḍā is an anklet similar to *panjeb* except that here no hollowed beads appear to the outer edges, but instead each knitted wire ends into a decorative design of very small discs. A pair of it weighs about 360 to 600 grams of silver.

Jhānjhar is a hollowed pipe of silver moulded into the form of an anklet without joining the two ends. It has a thicker body at the centre which gradually narrows down towards the ends. The hollowed pipe contains solid pieces of any metal, which produce sound on each step. A pair of this ornament weighs about 200 to 250 grams of silver.

Shākuntlā-chain is a thin knitted strap of silver having small drops. Its pair weighs about 60 to 100 grams. This ornament is called *ghuṇgru* in Pāngi area.

Paṭḍi or *paṭri*, as the name suggests, is a 3 to 4 cms wide strap of silver prepared by knitting together the numerous silver wires. It has two clasps to tie it around the ankles. Sometimes hollowed balls (*jhumkās*) are fixed by hooks to the lower border of this ornament. A pair of it weighs about 250 grams.

Ghunkaḍai is probably the heaviest of all the ornaments hitherto discussed. They are so heavy that it is difficult for the Gaddans to walk a long distance wearing them. This perhaps gave rise to the view maintained by Gaddis that the women were supposed to work as a house-wife within the confines of a house only. *Ghunkaḍai* are made of *kut* metal (bell metal) or brass. They are crude and rough and the solid mass of metal is hammered to fashion the ankelets by Rehāḍās, who specialise in the work of this sort of metal. The anklet is secured to the ankle by means of a big clasp. A pair of *ghunkaḍai* weighs not less than a kilogram. The *kut* is a very delicate metal liable to break into pieces once dropped from hand.

Saglā is also an ornament like *ghunkaḍai* but it is smaller in shape and lighter in weight (250 grams) and has no clasps. Both the ornaments are disappearing because of changing times, and it is cumbersome to wear them.

2. Ornaments for Toes

Phullu is a silver ring showing a motif of a petalled flower on its face. Another variety appears in the form of a ring with a bezel box which is inset with a bright coloured glass. A few *jhumkās* which jingle are also attached to it. A pair of *phullu* weighs about 25 to 30 grams.

Chhallā is a thin strip of silver coiled into 3 or 4 rolls. It weighs about 20 to 25 grams. A woman usually wears it for her husband's long life.

Guṭhaḍā is a silver ring for the big toe, with a triangular formation on it. This pointed triangular space is studded with round coloured small stones. It weighs around 25 grams. It is sometimes made in round shape also. It is said that *guṭhaḍā* protects one from abdominal or rheumatic pains.

Porḍi is shaped into the form of a ring by joining together the two opposite corners of a small square piece of metal in such a way that the ring bears the shape of a lozenge. The surface of the *porḍi* is dotted with various designs. Sometimes an almond-shaped silver disc is attached to the ring. Sometimes few *jhumkās* are attached to it. It weighs about 10 to 12 grams.

3. Ornaments for Males

Bāle, a large ear ring, is a popular ornament for the males. The only decoration in it is the thin wire, which recoils around the ring covering half of its portion. This is prepared in gold and worn on the lobe of ear. At the centre of *bāle* dangles an almond-shaped *sabzā* stone. It weighs about 24 grams. It is also called *sabzā* in some areas of this district.

Nanti is a small round ear ring made of gold. It is thick in the centre, the thickness gradually narrows down towards the ends. After wearing it in the lobe of the ears the two ends are compressed with *sansi.* It weighs from 12 to 24 grams. *Murki* is a small ear ring of gold into which are threaded few pearls. *Murki* weighs from 3 to 4 grams.

Dur is made by recoiling a single piece of wire into many circles. It weighs about 10 grams. The upper coil is in the form of a hook which is fixed to the lobe of the ear.

Kangṇū, nant, sabihi, kanṭhā, tabeet and *nām* are some other ornaments which in old times were worn by the menfolk of Chamba also. Gujjars invariably wear *tabeet.* But now with the advent of modern times and with the change in the dress habits these ornaments are no longer in vogue. *Janter, anguṭhi* and *chhallā* continue to be the popular ornaments of men in this district. The Gaddis still love to wear these ornaments besides *auttars*.

Buttons: Four silver buttons are linked with silver chain and are used by both men and women for buttoning up the holes of their shirts. Buttons come in many designs and shapes. From the uppermost button are suspended three chains which stop short at the middle button. From the middle button again emerge three similar chains, which run the length of the lower most button. At the end of the lowermost button a triangular plaque or a set of silver balls (*jhumkās*) is made to hang. The complete set of buttons roughly weighs 36 to 48 grams. The buttons are in the form of a dumb bell in shape, i.e. two round discs linked to a narrow neck in between.

The cuff-links are similar to silver buttons in design and shape. A small cluster of hollowed globular beads are also linked to it. These are also called studs. A pair of it weighs about 15 grams of silver.

4. Other Decorative Pieces

Mālā in fact is common generic name applied to all sorts of necklaces, but *mālā* here also connotes a particular necklace, which is made of stones like *mugā* (*mungā*) or *ṭuk*, *pherozā*, *ratti* and *chilkaṇu* or *alāk* or *moti* etc. *Rupānke* (silver beads) are also used in some kinds of *mālās*. In certain areas of Chamba a three or four-stringed *mālā* made of coloured stones is worn close to the neck. In olden days *mālā* made from *ṭuk-mugā* in four strings from which attached a silver *attar-dāni* or a scent-container was worn by both men and women. *Attar-dāni* is suspended by a silver chain and is decorated with *meenā*-work.

Hatholi is a wristlet made of a beaded thread having two or three rolls.

The women of Chamba also apply *ṭiklu* (*ṭikkā*) and *bindlu* (*bindi*) at the centre of their foreheads. The *ṭikkā* consists of a round looking-glass with some sort of dotted work done all around it. The diameter of the *ṭiklu* comes approximately close to 25 paisa coin. The *bindlu (bindi)* is made of a coloured glass and sometimes gold or silver leaf paper (*abari)* was cut into the size of a *bindi*. It is glued to the forehead by means of *sithā* (bees' wax). A Chamba woman now can buy these from the market.

The rings for fingers and the bangles for wrists were also at one time prepared from horse's hair and bamboo. Black and white horse tail-hairs were weaved around a ring of bamboo in such a way that a chess-board design appeared on the surface. The horsemen or saice of Chamba used to carry on this business when horses were the main sources of transportation.

Tattooing is also very common in this region, and there was a time when almost every hill woman and man had some sort of a tattoo mark on their body. Usually the tattooing is done in the fairs and festivals these days by the persons from outside, especially coming for that purpose. Some tribals indulged in the tattooing work themselves by piercing the skin with needle or thorn of a plant after dipping it in the juices extracted from wheat and barley plant. Sometimes *kājal* (mascara) obtained from the soot of the earthen plate placed on a *til*-oil earthen lamp-flame was also used as tattooing dye after mixing in into juices of wheat and barley plant. The most popular spots for tattooing among ladies have been the centre of the chin and on either sides of cheeks. Menfolk however, preferred tattooing in the form of flowers, rosettes and other motifs on their fleshy parts such as arms, upper arms and thighs probably to display their manhood. Tattooing of a star or a few dots on the chin has been a common fashion for the women-folk in these hills.

12

CONCLUSION

It is both fascinating and interesting to behold the varied and colourful pattern of life in the midst of nature. Over a long time, the people of Chamba in Himachal Pradesh have developed their own distinct way of life and living, customs and manners. To fight the sever cold all the year round and protect their bodies properly, they have developed technique of producing beautiful woollen cloth and their raw sensibility not failing them to invest these woollen lengths with design and colour combination of unmatched beauty.

Influences can be traced to far-flung places, for example, the style of wearing *chādru* or *khesh* (sheet) on the shoulder and torso and *suthan* (trousers) by the Pāngi women resembles the style and manner in which it is worn by the women of Kullu region of Himachal Pradesh. Kullu women tie a piece of cloth around their head called *dhāṭhu*, whereas, cobra-hooded cap known as *joji* loved by the women of Pāngi and Churāh is akin to the flat cap worn by the Hunza women of Hindukush and Kurdish women of Persia.

Over the centuries people belonging to different tribal and racial stock have come together and mixed in the mainstream of life of this hilly region. In Chamba, we find the mixture of different culture groups whose beliefs, myths and legends as also the fashions in dress and ornaments have become manifest in the broad spectrum of culture.

The dress habits have relevance to the religious beliefs and faith of people. Woollen cloth is regarded pure and sacred and dress prepared from woollen cloth is worn when the ritual of *sharadh* is to be performed. During the days after death in the family and during the menstrual period of a woman if woollen cloth is used it may not be washed in water, since woollen cloth is considered as pure. Some *gangājal* or cow-dung water is sprinkled on it and that is enough. It was a custom during the olden days, that in the community feast, menfolk would partake of food only wearing a *dhoti* or woollen garments. Clothes made of cotton were not allowed to be worn during the feast. The priests attending to the rituals connected with a temple were supposed to wear only woollen garments in olden days, these being pure and sacred garments. In the days gone-by when one donned proper traditional dress made of woollen cloth he was looked upon with respect and given preference. Dress constituted main factor in enhancing the prestige of a person. The occasions when such dress was worn were marriage, fair and festival or some other happy and auspicious day.

Times are now changing, economy of poorer classes is taking turn. Agriculture has become lucrative due to the introduction of cash crops. People on the whole are now shedding heavy woollen garments and thick silver jewellery and are taking to the trendy fashions of towns in the manner of dress and jewellery. Accessibility to far-flung places and their getting connected with buses and cars have speeded up this transformation. With the new riches people have become enterprising and they are shifting their establishments on to the newly purchased lands. The Gaddis of Brahmour have settled in the plains of Kangra and needless to say they are adopting the dress, ornaments, food habits and language of their newly acquired neighbours. The same is true of Pangwālās who have now settled in large number at Chamba.

The life-style of Gujjars has also undergone a great change. Instead of leading a nomadic life and rearing cattle, they have taken to agriculture which requires settled life. Of late they have become serious about their religion and are copying fashions of other Islamic countries like Pakistan. Under the current of change that is sweeping over lies the factors like education, expansion of means of transportation, new outlook, television, telephones etc. and a feeling of weariness with traditional ways of life. Whether this change is for the good or whether this will ruin our age-old traditions, only time will tell.

In the meantime it is interesting to see a village belle wearing terelyn suit and lads wearing bell-bottom and heavy shoes. Such ready-made stuff is easy to buy from the market, given the better financial status. Tribals who are in jobs and have recently moved to big towns and cities now find rough woollen cloth irritating to their skin.

Now the modern market is full of fake jewellery, which is gaudy, glittering and cheap and has the capacity to attract the customers with its sparkle. Any woman will naturally fall prey to this kind of imitation ornaments which are cheap, have a great variety and are available for throw-away prices. The rural people are now selling their old heavy and old-fashioned ornaments of silver to goldsmiths, and in return, they are going in for lighter and modern designed jewellery of gold and silver.

The change is widespread and sweeping the countryside at a fast rate swallowing the traditional modes. Change in attitudes and trends is reflected in the following lines from a popular folk song of Chamba:

"Gāḍā jo minjar[1] *bhnāi ho—terālin sūṭ lai ai ho."*

The singer of this couplet is a tribal beauty, who has presented a *minjar* to her suitor, a forest guard in that region. The forest guard in return has presented her with a fine terelyn suit. Here it will not be inappropriate to mention another song of Chamba which was popular in this region, when the new trends and the changes in the fashion had not taken place. This song runs like this:

"Lāl terā sāfā bhaurā, maure keri kalgi ho,
chiṭā terā cholā bhaurā, mano rā katorā ho,
lakā tere ḍorā bhaurā, baṇi baṇi pundā ho."

1. Minjar is a beautiful bunch of *gotā* and *zari* tied in the button-holes a full week before Minjar fair of Chamba, when it is ceremoniously immersed in the Ravi river by the whole populace that goes to the river banks in a royal procession. Minjar is presented in Chamba to nearer and dearer ones, and even to the local and family deities.

Here now the Gaddan damsel is head over heels in love with young Gaddi named Bhaurā. In the couplet the Gaddan admires the charming and beautiful Gaddi dress and *sāfā* which Bhaurā wears with a *kalgi* (plume) of a peacock decorating his turban.

The culture of Chamba is pristine, pure and well preserved on the high hills, but now it is going to be diluted and in certain cases discarded in favour of wider regional and national way of life, which is neither unnatural nor undesirable.

Appendix 1. Tribes and People of Chamba

Tehsil	Generic term	Tribes/People	Clan	Caste	Dialects
1. Bhaṭṭiyāt	Bhaṭṭiyāl	1. Gaddi tribe	Hindu	Brahmin, Rajput, Aryas, Sipi	Bhaṭeāli
		2. Others (Hindu & Mohammedan)		Hali, Koli, Harijan, Khatri, Mahājan, Dhogri, Ḍhobis, Mahāshyās, Ḍoomnās	Bhaṭeāli-Bharmouri or Gādī
		3. Gurkha	Hindu	Brahmin, Rajput and other castes	Gorkhāli or Nepali
		4. Gujjar tribe	Mohammedan	Musalman	Gujjari
2. Brahmour	Gaddi	1. Gaddi tribe	Hindu	Brahmin, Rajput, Aryas, Sipi, Hāli, Koli, Khatri etc.	Bharmouri or Gādī, Gādī-Hindi
		2. Gujjar tribe	Mohammedan	Musalman	Gujjari
3. Chamba	Chamyāl or Chambyāl	1. Gaddi tribe (in upper Ravi valley and in adjoining villages)	Hindu	Ad-dharmi, Aryas, Brahmins, Mahāshyās, Mahājan, Rajput, Khatri, Rāṭhi, Betwal, Hāli, Sipi, Koli, Ḍoomnās, Harijan etc.	Chameālī, Dogri, Gādī-Chameālī, Gādī-Hindi
		2. Others (Hindu & Mohammedan)		—	—
		3. Gujjars	Mohammedan	Musalman	Gujjari

(Contd.)

Appendix 1 continued

Tehsil	Generic term	Tribes/People	Clan	Caste	Dialects
		4. Pārāchanāri (displaced persons from frontier province of undivided Punjab)	Hindu	Brahmin, Khatri etc.	Pārāchanāri, Chameālī
4. Churāh	Churāhī	1. Gaddi tribes	Hindu	As above	Churāhī
		2. Others (Hindu & (Mohammedan)		As above	Churāhī-Gādī
		3. Bushehari	Hindu/ Buddhist	Rajput, Brahmins & other Scheduled castes	Busheharī, Churāhī, Churāhī-Bushehari
		4. Gujjar tribe	Mohammedan	Musalman	Gujjari
5. Pāngi	Pangwālā	1. Pangwālā tribe	Hindu	Brahmin, Rajput, Aryas, Sipi, Hāli, Khatri etc.	Pangwāli, (Lahuli in Chamba-Lahul)
		2. Bhoṭ tribe (60-70 families)	Buddhist	—	Bhoṭiā

Appendix 2. Costumes Worn by Inhabitants of Different Tehsils of Chamba

Tehsils	Part of body	Costume	
		Female	Male
1	2	3	4
1. Bhaṭṭiyāt			
(a) Bhaṭṭiyāl	Head	Hariḍā (dupaṭṭā) Gokhruwālā or Sādā, Chādru	Sāfā, Ṭopi
	Torso	Kurtā Kaliwālā, Kameej	Kameej Sādā or Kalidār, Coat, Bāsket
	Lower limb (undergarments)	Chuḍidār Suthan, Shalwār Phairdār, Ghagri	Pyjāmā, Paḍtaṇi (Dhoti)
	Foot	Juṭṭi, Chappal etc.	Juṭṭi, Juṭṭā, Chappal. Paḍtaṇi used as Sāfā. Chādar used as Shawl
(b) Gurkhas	Head	Rumāl	Nepali Ṭopi
	Torso	Blouse	Kameez (white long shirt), Coat, Daurā, Vascoat black
	Lower limb	Sāri	Pyjāmā Chuḍidār, Paṭukā (Kamar-paṭṭā white)
2. Brahmour	Head	Dupaṭṭā, Ghunḍu Dhankāwālā, Sādā or Goṭhṇiwālā	Sāfā, Ṭop
	Torso	Kameej, Choli or Cholu (woollen), Luanchaḍi (cotton), Ḍorā (Gātri)	Kurtā, Cholā, Choli, Khaptān, Ḍorā (Gātri)
	Lower limb (undergarments)	Suthan Chuḍidār	Suthan, Pyjāmā
	Foot	Mochḍi, Mochḍu	Juṭṭā

(Contd.)

1	2	3	4
3. Chamba	Head	Gokhruwālā Dupaṭṭā, Goṭhṇiwālā Dupaṭṭā, Dhankāwālā Dupaṭṭā, Sādā Dupaṭṭā	Sāfā, Pagḍi
	Torso	Kameej, Kurtā (Kaliwālā without collar or Sādā with collar and cuff), Peshwāj (Sādā or Gotewāli), Cholu, (woollen)	Kameej, Coat, Bāsket, Chogā, Jāmā, Angarkhi, Lak (Paṭkā), Dupaṭṭā or Chādar used as 'utri' or Shawl
	Lower limb (undergarments)	Suthan Chuḍidār (loose or fit)	Suthan Gulbadan ki Chuḍidār, Pyjāmā tang ponchewālā
		Sāri, Suit (Salwār, Shirt and Dupaṭṭā), Shawl etc.	Sāfā, Kameej, Coat, Pyjāmā, western dress etc.
	Foot	Juṭṭi (Sādā, Tillewāli, Resham-wāli), modern shoes etc.	Juṭṭā (Tillewālā or Sādā), modern shoes etc.
4. Churāh	Head	Joji, Dupaṭṭā	Sāfā, Ṭop
	Torso	Kameej, Bāsket, Paṭkā	Kameej, Cholā, Ḍorā, Coat, Bāsket
	Lower limb	Ḍoḍ, Chuḍyāli	Suthan, Pyjāmā
	Foot	Paṇi, Chappal, Juṭṭā	Juṭṭā
5. Pāngi			
(a) Pangwālā	Head	Joji	Ṭop, Sāfā
	Torso	Choli, Kameej, Chādru or Khesh	Kamari, Kameej, Long Coat (Chogā), Koṭh, Mājhin
	Lower limb	Chālaṇ	Chālaṇ woollen and cotton
	Foot	Pulān, Juṭṭā	Pulān, Juṭṭā

(Contd.)

1	2	3	4
(b) Bhot	–	(Both male and female) Shirt, Chuḍidār Pyjāmā woollen, Cholā woollen (Long gown reaching upto ankles in special design)	
	Forehead	Joji, Dupaṭṭā	Ṭopi
6. Gujjar	Head	Joji, Jhoomb	Sāfā
	Torso	Kurtā Kalidār	Bangali Kameej, Kalidār Kurtā, Bāsket
	Lower limb (undergarments)	Suthan Chuḍidār	Themat, Ghuṭanā Silwār (Shalwār)
	Head and upper body	Salārā and Neelak used for wrapping around the head and upper portion of the body	Poti, Khaisi (Chādar) used as Shawl
	Foot	Desi Juṭṭi by both male and female	

Appendix 3. Ornaments Worn by Different People and Tribes of Chamba

Tehsil and people	Part of body	Ornament	
		Female	Male
1	2	3	4
1. Bhaṭṭiyāt			
(a) Bhaṭṭiyāl	Head	Chaunk	
	Forehead	Singārpaṭṭi, Ṭikkā, Chandru, Chiḍi	—
	Ear	Bāli, Jhumku, Small ear rings in projection of the ear, Karaṇphul	Nanti
	Nose	Besar, Nath, Long, Balāk, Tili, Kokā	—
	Neck	Bugdi, Kanṭhā, Ḍoḍmālā, Rānihār	Kanṭhā, Jantar
	Wrist	Toke, Bangā, Chuḍā, Mareḍri, Kangṇū	—
	Fingers	Anguṭhi, Chhallā	Anguṭhi, Chhallā
	Ankel	Panjeb, Paṭri, Shakuntlā Chain, Saglā (outdated)	—
	Toe	Chhallā, Porḍi, Guṭhaḍā	—
(b) Gurkha tribe	Head	Seerphul, Mangṭikā, Singārpaṭṭi	—
	Ear	Mārūḍi, Bāle	—
	Nose	Phulli, Nath, Kokā	—
	Neck	Tillhār (Mangal Sutar), Teepmālā, Hār etc.	—
	Wrist	Chuḍi, Bangā	—
	Fingers	Ring, Anguṭhi	Ring, Anguṭhi
	Ankel	Pajeeb (like Shakuntlā Chain)	—
2. Brahmour Gaddi (tribe)	Head	Chaunk, Chaukphulu	—
	Forehead	Chiḍi, Manṭikā, Janjeer	—

(Contd.)

1	2	3	4
	Ears	Phair, Jhumku, Bāli, Chhiku, Pharālu, Ḍaḍku	Murki, Nanti, Dur, Bāle
	Nose	Long, Bālu, Nathli, Nath, Balāk	—
	Neck	Jaumālā, Ḍoḍmālā, Chamkali, Galsari (out dated), Kanḍhu, Chanderhār, Sabihi, Auttar, Nāḍi, Jantar	Kanṭhā, Sabihi, Tabeet, Jantar, Nāḍi, Singi
	Wrist	Ṭoke, Kangṇū, Bangā, Chhaṇ-Kangṇū, Borāwāli-Bang	Kangṇū
	Fingers	Anguṭhi, Chhallā	Anguṭhi, Chhallā
	Ankel	Ghunkaḍai (out dated), Panjeb, Shakuntlā Chain, Saglā etc.	—
	Toe	Phullu, Porḍi	—
		Ornamental Decorative Pieces	
		Mālā: Made of Mugā (ṭuk) Rupānke (beads of silver), Pherozā Ratti etc. (worn by both male and female).	
		Kundal: Feathers of birds fixed with hairs above the ears by ladies.	
		Buttons: Of silver with chain used in shirts by both men and women.	
		Chhaṭṭā: Consists of a rounded mirror fixed on a small circular piece made of goat skin and is decorated all around with Rattis used by both male and female.	
3. Chamba Chambyāi	Head	Chaunk-Phul, Singārpaṭṭi Jhaṭpaṭṭu	—
	Forehead	Mantikā (Mangtikā) Arg-Chandru (Chandra), Jhumar	—
	Ear	Bāli, Kan-Chhiku, Jhumku, Karṇphul, Pharālu, Kanṭā, Ṭops, Rings, Bundai	Bāli & Nanti
	Nose	Bālu, Balu (Chuṭkiwālā), Bulāk (Balāk) Chhikāiwali, Balākḍu, Long, Kunḍe (rings with leaves), Tilli, Nath, Bisar, Phuli	—

(Contd.)

1	2	3	4
	Neck	Nām, Ḍoḍmālā, Gulband, Chamkali, Sabihi, Hār (Chanderhār or Satlaḍi Hār) Gunj, Kanṭhā, Chauki, Bugdī, Mālā	Kanṭhā, Tabeet, Nām, Jantar, Nāḍi
	Wrist	Kangṇū, Ghokharu, Maredaḍi, Ṭoke, Ponchhi, Chhaṇ-Kangaṇ, Bangā (gold), Chuḍi (Churi)	Kangṇū
	Upper arm	Bazuband, Nant, Pariband	Nant, Jantar
	Fingers	Anguṭhi, Nahastrā, Chhallā, Arsi, Rings	Anguṭhi, Chhallā, Ring
	Ankel	Panjeb (Pazeb), Sādā Ṭoḍā, Ṭodā, Jhānhar, Paṭḍi, Shakuntlā Chain	—
	Toes	Phullu, Guṭhaḍā, Bechhwa (same as Guṭhaḍā)	—
		Decorative Pieces	
		Kundal, Mālā of jems	Mālā of Ṭuk and Alāk
		Buttons: Of silver with chain used in shirts by both men and women	
4. Churāh Churāhīs	Forehead	Mangṭikā (rare), Shangli	—
	Ears	Karaṇphul, Bāli, Kālu (5 to 6 in the pinna)	Nanti, Bālā
	Nose	Long, Nathli, Bulāk, Tilli, Ṭiki, Murki	—
	Neck	Ḍoḍmālā, Sabihi, Hār	Kanṭhā, Sabihi, Jantar, Singi, Nāḍi
	Wrist	Ṭoke, Kangṇū, Chhaṇ-bangā	Kangṇū
	Fingers	Anguṭhi, Mundri	Anguṭhi, Mundri
	Ankel	Jhanjhar, Panjeb	—
	Toe	Phullu	—

(Contd.)

1	2	3	4
		Other Decorative Pieces	
		Mālā of Alāk and Ṭuk for neck	
		Buttons: Of silver with chain, worn by both men and women	
5. Pāngi Pangwālā tribe	Head	Janjeer	—
	Ear	Kālu, Sankli with Jhumku, Tilli, Ḍeḍku	Nanti, (Bekhali)
	Nose	Phuli, Long, Balāk (Balākh, Murki), Tiki	—
	Neck	Ḍoḍmālā, Dūssar, Tabik (Tabeet), Kanṭhḍu (Kanṭhā)	Kanṭhā
	Wrist	Bang, Haroḍu (Kangṇū)	—
	Fingers	Anguṭhi, Mundri	Anguṭhi, Mundri
	Ankel	Silver Panjeb, Shakuntlā Chain (only in Bhain Chaḍi area are called Ghuṇgru)	—
	Toes	Phullu	—
6. Gujjar tribe	Forehead	Chiḍi was worn sometimes ago	—
	Ear	Bālian (Gol), Kanbāle	—
	Nose	Long, Nathli (Murki), Ṭiki	—
	Neck	Hanseeri (Hansli), Tabeet, Ḍoḍmālā, Mhail (Hamail)	Tabeet
	Wrist	Kangṇū, Ṭoke	—
	Fingers	Mundri, Challā, Anguṭhi	Mundri, Chhallā, Anguṭhi
	Ankel	Nil	—
	Toe	Nil	—

Appendix 4. Costumes in Pahāḍi Paintings

In the Pahāḍi paintings of Chamba as well as of other north-western hill states of the region, for the period from mid-18th to mid-19th century, it is observed that the costume of women was *choli, ghāgrā* and *oḍhni*. This dress in some other form is also shown worn by the earliest image of Lakshnā Devi at Brahmour in Chamba (7th century A.D.). This type of dress in its earliest form seems to be of Central Asian origin. To quote Hermann Goetz:

> "The Rajput type of costume, though later adopted by the Mughals and, thus, spread over the whole of India, is also originally non-Indian. The female "ballerina" skirt and the male short, pointed (quadrangular) shirt with a waist hole, in the centre, as well as the tunic with a neck hole, must be derivatives from tranian costumes first depicted on the reliefs of the Achaemenian kings. There also the later Rajput and Mughal jāmā (knee-long-coat fastened under one shoulder) first appears; later it was introduced into India by the Sakas and continued to be the fashion throughout the Middle Ages, as is shown by the coins."[1]

The *shalwār* and *kameej* appear in the Chamba paintings during Sikh period, hence, this costume seems to have travelled to the hills from Punjab to Chamba in the early 19th century. The *sāri* is a modern transformation of the old *choli, ghāgrā* and *ḍupaṭṭā* and came into fashion around 1780 A.D., but the hilly women did not adopt the costume even till the present time. In the whole of India, Chamba appears to be the only region where *peshwāj* of the Mughal period is still seen to be in use. A decade or two ago *peshwāj* was very much in vogue. From the painting also we gather that womenfolk of those times used to keep their hair untied and use to comb them into interlacing plaits or tie them into buns. They used fancy things of make-up like *sandal, kājal, sindur, chandan, tilāk* and *henna* etc. and used to keep these in a sliding wooden box.

The ornaments of choice were *gulband, bajuband, kangaṇ, sheshphul, karaṇphul, nath, arsi, anguṭhi, anguṭhḍā* and *pajeb (panjeb)*.

The nobles and the kings portrayed in these Pahāḍi paintings are frequently shown wearing *nantis* studded with diamonds. Raja Umed Singh (1748-1764 A.D.), Raja Prithvi Singh (1641-1664 A.D.), Raja Chattar Singh (1664-1690 A.D.) and Wazir Bagha (1808-1844) wear ear ornaments in these paintings.

The men of Chamba used to wear *jāmā, paṭkā* and *suthan*. The headgear was the Mughal turban. However, while the *choli, ghāgrā* and *dupaṭṭā* has occasionally been found in the old houses of Chamba, but the authors have not come across any old Mughal dress.

1. Hermann Goetz, *Art and Architecture of Bikaner State*, Oxford (1950), p. 121.

The size and the form of the *jāmā* of men used to change from time to time according to the dress popular in the Mughal court at Delhi. In the Pahāḍi style paintings the *jāmās* of the reign of Farrukh-Syyar and Mohammad Shah were popular while in the Basholi paintings the *jāmās* of Aurangzeb's period are seen. The *jāmās* of Farrukh-Syyar and Mohammad Shah during mid-18th century are multi-pleated and fall up to the ankles, and even women are shown wearing this type of dress in these paintings. They are even turbaned in the male fashion sometimes, but this dress seems to be confined to the Royal ladies only.

References

Books in English

1. Crook, William, *Religion and Folk Lore of Northern India*, New Delhi, 1925.
2. Cunningham, Alexander, *Archaeological Survey of India*, Simla, 1871.
3. Dutta, Bhupindra Nath, *Indian Art in Relation to Culture*, Calcutta, 1978.
4. Dey, Nundo Lal, *Geographical Dictionary of an Ancient and Medieval India*, New Delhi, 1971.
5. Fabri, Charles Louis, *Indian Dress—A Brief History*, New Delhi, 1960.
6. Goetz, Hermann, *Art and Architecture of Bikaner State*, Oxford, 1950.
7. Goetz, Hermann, *Early Wooden Temples of Chamba*, Netherlands, 1955.
8. Goetz, Hermann, *Studies in the History and Art of Kashmir and the Indian Himalaya*, Wiesbaden, 1969.
9. Goetz, Hermann, *Rajput Art and Architecture*, edited by Joytindra Jain and Jutta Jain, Wiesbaden, 1978.
10. Hutchison, J. and Vogel, J.P.H., *History of the Punjab Hill States*, Vol. I, Labore, 1933.
11. Negi, Thakur Sen, *District Gazetteer of Chamba*, 1963.
12. Negi, Thakur Sen, *Scheduled Tribes of Himachal Pradesh: A Profile*, Meerut, 1976.
13. Newell, William H., *Report on Scheduled Castes and Scheduled Tribes, Census of India*, 1961.
14. Ohri, V.C., *Art of Himachal,* State Museum, Simla, 1975.
15. Sharma, Tej Ram, *Ancient Tribes of Himachal Pradesh, Himachal Art and Archaeology*, edited by Dr. V.C. Ohri, State Museum, Simla, 1980.
16. Singh, R.C. Paul, *A Village Survey*, Brahmour, 1961.

Books in Hindi

1. Agrawala, Vasudev Sharn, *Pāṇini Kaleen Bhāratvarsh*, Banaras, 2012 Vik.
2. Sankrityayan, Rahul, *Ṛgvedic Arya*, Allahabad, 1957.

Papers and Magzines

1. Puri, B.N., Chamba under Gurjara Pratihars, Research Paper.
2. *Marg*, Vol. XXXIII, No. I.

INDEX

alāk 118
angarkhā 77
anguṭhi 114, 117
argh-chandru 77
arsi (*arsu*) 113
attar-dāni 118
aṭṭi 51
Audumbaras 29, 35, 75
Aurangzeb 32, 33, 56, 79
auttars 108, 118

bāgh-nakh 93
baglu 51
bajuband 94, 110, 111
bak-suā 37
balāk 102
balākḍu 102
bāli (*bale*) 98, 117
bālu 100, 101, 102
bang 113
bāsket 60, 71, 73
baṭṭu 51
besār 100, 101
Bharmouri (Gādī) 47
Bhaṭṭiyālans 86
Bhaṭṭiyāls 83
Bhaṭṭiyāt 27, 35, 83, 84, 98, 107, 129
Bhoṭs 65, 68
bhujlu 51, 52
Bhuri Singh, Raja 34, 40, 41, 42
bindi (*bindlu*) 118, 119

bores 112
Brahmour 27, 28, 29, 30, 34, 35, 37, 40, 42, 43, 44, 46, 63, 71, 96
Buddhists 68
bugdī 108
bunḍe 98, 100
Bushehar 74
Bushehari ṭopi 74
Busheharis 69, 70
butki 108

chādar (*chaddar*) 39, 61, 62, 77, 85
chādru 67, 68, 72, 86
chālaṇ (*chālar*) 65, 67
Chamba 18, 19, 21, 22, 27, 28, 32, 34, 35, 37
Chamba *chappal* 79, 82, 85, 86
Chambyāls 75
Chameālī 48
chamkali 104
chander-hār 107
chaunk 95
Central Asia 64, 69
chhallā 113, 116, 117
chhan-kangaṇ 112
chhaṭṭā 54
chhiku 98
chiḍi 96
chilkaṇu 118
chogā 66, 78
cholā, choli 49, 50, 51, 52, 66, 71, 77

choli (*cholu/choie*) 40, 49, 53, 54, 55, 67, 73, 79, 80, 81, 86
cholu 55, 80
chuḍa 111
chuḍi 113
chuḍidār pyjāmā 42, 60, 65, 66, 78
chuḍyāli 74
Churāh 27, 35, 36, 64, 66, 98
Churāhans 39, 72, 97
Churāhis 36, 69, 70
chuṭki 101
Cloth-making 37
Costumes of Bhaṭṭiyālans 86, 126
Costumes of Bhaṭṭiyāls 85, 126
Costumes of Brahmour 126
Costumes of Chambyālans 79, 127
Costumes of Chambyāls 76, 127
Costumes of Churāhans 72, 127
Costumes of Churāhis 70, 127
Costumes of Gaddans 53
Costumes of Gaddis 48
Costumes of Gujjaris 61, 128
Costumes of Gujjars 59, 128
Costumes of Gurkhas 87, 126
Costumes of Pahāḍi paintings 133
Costumes of Pangwālans 67, 127
Costumes of Pangwālās 65, 127
Cunningham, Alexander 45, 56

daurā 87
Decorative pieces 118
ḍedku (*ḍhodku*) 99
ḍhaḍi 109
Dhaula-Dhār 27, 28
ḍhol 109
ḍoḍ 39, 73
ḍoḍā 104
ḍoḍ-mālā 104, 105
ḍorā (*ḍori*) 49, 50, 51, 52, 54, 71, 95
dupaṭṭā 53, 54, 72, 80, 86
dur 117
Dutta, Bhupendra Nath 37, 39

Exhibitionism 15-16

Footwear of Chambyālans 82
Footwear of Chambyāls 79
Footwear of Churāhans 74
Footwear of Churāhis 71
Footwear of Gaddans 55
Footwear of Gaddis 52
Footwear of Gujjaris 62

Gaddans 53-55
Gaddis 21, 36, 37, 40, 44
  dog of 47
  land of 46
  origin of 44
  way of life 46
galpaṭṭu 105
galsāri (*galsri*) 105
garkhi 77
gātri 50, 51, 54, 74
ghāgrā (*ghāgri*) 36, 79, 81, 86
ghunḍu 53, 54
ghunghaṭ 53
ghungrālu 93
ghuṇgrus 96, 116
ghunkaḍai 116
ghuṭanā 60
Goetz, Hermann 21, 29, 30, 36, 45, 63
gōjru 111
gokhrū 111
goṭṭā 53, 54, 74, 78, 80, 81, 82
Gujjaris 61
Gujjars 21, 56,
  life-style of 57
gulbadan 82
gunj 107
Gurjara-Pratihara 21, 30, 31, 56, 63
Gurkha women 87, 99
Gurkhas (Nepalis) 87, 96
guṭhaḍā 117

hamail 94, 108
hanseeri 107
hansli 94, 107, 108
hār 92
hariḍā 86

hatholi 118
Head-dress of Churāhans 72
Head-dress of Churāhīs 70
Head-dress of Gaddans 53
Head-dress of Gaddis 48
Head-dress of Gujjaris 61

Indo-Scythian dresses 21, 29, 41

jaḍulā 37, 53
jāmā 41, 42, 76
janjeeri (*janjeer*) 92, 96, 97
jantar 108, 110, 117
Jatras 53, 71, 92
jau-mālā 104
Jewellery 91-93
jhānjhar 115
jhaṭpaṭṭu 96
jhoomb 61
jhumar 98
jhumkās (*jhamku*) 95, 96, 99, 104, 106, 112, 115, 117, 118
joji 61, 67, 72, 97
juṭṭā 52, 55, 62, 71, 74, 85
juṭṭi 55, 82, 87

kāḍu 99
kājal 119
kalgi 48
kālū 98
kamar-band 66, 74
kamari 65
kamar-paṭṭā 87
kambalā 35
kameej 52, 55, 60, 65, 71, 73, 81, 82, 86
kan-chhiku 99
kanḍhapu-ṭopi 48
kanḍhṇu 105
kanḍhu 108
kangṇū 111, 112, 117
kānṭā (*kanṭe*) 98, 100
kanṭhā 105, 117
kanṭhḍu 105
kanṭop 48, 59, 71
karaṇ-phul 96, 99
khaisi 61
khaptān 49, 50
Khāśas 29, 30
khesh 67
kokā 93, 103
kokh 49
Kolis 29, 30
koṭh 66
kunḍā (*kunḍi*) 103
kunḍhu 93
kurtā 52, 60, 61, 82, 85
Kushāna art 29

likkaḍ (*likkar*) 66
long 103
luanchḍi 54

maikhal 39
mājhin 66
mālā 94, 107, 118
mangal-sutra 107
manṭikkā (*ṭikkā*) 96, 97
maredaḍi 111
Maru, Raja 31, 34, 39
mārūḍi 99
meenā-work 112
mhail (*hamail*) 94, 108
mochḍi 55
mochḍu 55
moti 51, 118
mugā (*mungā*) 118
Mughal costumes 33, 41, 42
mundri 114
murki 93, 103, 104, 117

nādi 109
nag 103
nahastra 113
nām 105, 117
nant 110, 117
nanti 94, 117
nath 101, 102

nathli 103, 104
nazar-baṭṭu 93
neelak 62

oḍhani 81
Ohri, V.C. 40, 78
Ornaments for ankels 115
Ornaments for ears 98
Ornaments for fingers 113
Ornaments for head 95
Ornaments for males 117
Ornaments for neck 104
Ornaments for nose 100
Ornaments for toes 116
Ornaments for upper arms 110
Ornaments for wrists 110
Ornaments of Bhaṭṭiyāt 129
Ornaments of Brahmour 129
Ornaments of Chamba 130
Ornaments of Churāh 131
Ornaments of Gujjar 132
Ornaments of Pāngi 132

paḍtaṇi 85
pagḍi 48, 77
Pahāḍi style 94
pājeb (panjeb) 115
Pāngi 18, 27, 35, 36, 37, 63, 64, 98, 99, 105
Pangwālans 67
Pangwālās 36, 37, 63
paṇi 71, 74, 79, 82
Pārāchanāris 76
paṭḍi 116
paṭkā 40, 50, 66, 71, 73, 74, 77
paṭṭu 38, 49, 50, 54, 67, 70, 79, 80
paṭṭu-suthan 55
paṭṭukā 87
pendal 106
peshwāj 36, 54, 79, 80
phair 98
pharālu 99
pherozā 113, 114, 118
phulli 93, 103
phullu 96, 116
Pir Panjāl 27, 63
ponchhi 112
porḍi 117
poti 61
puhālas 49
pulā 67
pulāns (pullay) 66, 74
pusān 35
pyjāmā 52, 60, 66, 71, 74. 77, 82, 85, 87

rajuḍ 37
rālū 109
Ranas 34
rani-hār 107
ratti 54, 118
Rehāḍās 37, 93, 111, 116
rehāḍu 93
rumāl 88, 92
ruṇkā 51
rupānke 118

sabihi (sabhi) 106, 117
sabzā 105, 117
sāfā 48, 59, 70, 77, 78
sagla 116
Sahila Varman 32, 34, 40, 75
salārā 62
saṇān 37
sanghaṭi 68
sangli 51
sānkali (sangḍi) 99
sansi 117
saraṇ 69
sāri 81, 82, 88
satlaḍi-hār 106, 107
seli 51
Shākuntlā-*chain* 115
shalwār 55, 60, 62, 82, 86
shangli 97, 99
singārpaṭṭi 96
singi 109

sipi 51
sirphoal 96
sithā 119
Śiva 29, 39, 43, 47, 91
Śiva-ri-seli 51
susi 62
suthan chuḍidār 52, 55, 62, 67, 71, 77, 88

tabeet 106, 117
Tattooing 119
ṭdāgi 93
teep-mālā 107
Thakurs & Ranas 30
thālch 37
themat 60
thewa 103
thobi 37, 64
ṭiki 101, 104
ṭikkā 96, 118, 119
ṭiklu (*ṭikkā*) 96, 118, 119
til-hār 107
tillā 79
tilli 98, 102, 103
toḍā 115
ṭokās 94
ṭoke 112
ṭop 48, 65, 70
ṭopi 49, 59, 61, 65, 74, 78, 87
ṭops 100
Tribes & people of Chamba 124
ṭuk 118

Vaṁśāvalī 31

Wazarat 35, 83
Wazir Bagha 34, 42
Woollen clothes 38

Zaskar 63